D0924750

Jan

The Youngest Woman Sentenced to Georgia's Death Row

NO LONGER PROPERTY OF
ANYTHINK LIBRARIES/
RANGEVIEW LIBRARY DISTRICT

JODI MCDANIEL LOWERY

outskirts press

The opinions expressed in this manuscript are solely the opinions of the author and do not represent the opinions or thoughts of the publisher. The author has represented and warranted full ownership and/or legal right to publish all the materials in this book.

Jan
The Youngest Woman Sentenced to Georgia's Death Row
All Rights Reserved.
Copyright © 2017 Jodi McDaniel Lowery
v2.0

Cover Photo © 2017 Janice Buttrum. All rights reserved - used with permission.

This book may not be reproduced, transmitted, or stored in whole or in part by any means, including graphic, electronic, or mechanical without the express written consent of the publisher except in the case of brief quotations embodied in critical articles and reviews.

Outskirts Press, Inc.
http://www.outskirtspress.com

ISBN: 978-1-4787-9049-5

Outskirts Press and the "OP" logo are trademarks belonging to Outskirts Press, Inc.

PRINTED IN THE UNITED STATES OF AMERICA

Acknowledgements

To my dad, Carlton McDaniel, who has supported me as I pursue this dream of being a writer, thank you for the unconditional love as I continue enjoying this journey.

To the people in law enforcement and our local judicial system who have shared their knowledge and stories of the Buttrums, thank you for being willing to share your stories and experiences. Your input has tremendously added to the story and your willingness to support a local author is truly inspiring.

To my friends and family, thank you for supporting me by purchasing my books, continuing to give me future ideas and for just being you. I am humbled to be recognized as an author.

To Judy Alred, I can't begin to put into words how much I appreciate you. You are my mistake finder, mentor, and most of all my friend. You help me to bring my stories to life.

Thank you for helping me become a better writer.

Finally, to my husband, my cheerleader, my promotor and my best friend, you ROCK!! Thank you for ALWAYS supporting me. Who knew you would marry a woman who went to prison voluntarily? I love you and a simple thank you just isn't enough.

Book Dedication

To my loving husband, Dale
My two children, Andrew and Lauren and
My five GRANDbabies, Lucas, Annelise, Aedyn, Ross and Thomas

Table of Contents

Author's Note

A good friend once told me that we are all here to be a witness to someone else's life. I never dreamed when I began this journey over a year ago, I would become a witness to the life of Janice Buttrum.

Janice was convicted of a horrendous murder in 1981 in the city of Dalton, Georgia, and became the youngest woman sentenced to death in the state. Her sentence would later be changed to three life sentences without parole. Now, after spending 36 years or over two-thirds of her life behind bars, that could change with her likely chance at being granted a parole hearing.

In the normal scheme of things, Janice's life and my life would probably have never crossed. I was raised in a home with two loving parents who were married over 57 years before my mom's death in 2013. I was the third of four children. I label myself the middle "rebellious" child, although I have never been in trouble with law enforcement except for the occasional speeding ticket. My siblings, two STAR students and a valedictorian, excelled in school, and then there was me; although now I hold multiple college degrees.

Janice, on the other hand, had a much more difficult life than I did. She was born to a prostitute mother, raised by alcoholic parents, and spent time in both foster care and juvenile centers. She was married at age fifteen to an abusive spouse and had her first child at sixteen. She participated in a horrific murder at seventeen and was pregnant with her second child at the time. By the age of eighteen, she was widowed and sitting on Georgia's death row.

I first started corresponding with Janice in January, 2016. As of this writing, we have exchanged over fifty letters. Some have been just brief notes while others have been several pages long. I have also spent almost forty hours with her face to face learning about her life.

People worried that I would be sympathetic to Janice because of her upbringing, but then I had to face the harsh reality that she took another person's life. In her first note to me, Janice asked me what I thought about the death penalty. To be honest, I wasn't really sure. My Southern Baptist upbringing made me think about the Old Testament teachings about an eye for an eye. On the other hand, I also knew about grace and God's forgiveness. Janice shared with me that she had become a Christian not long after her conviction. I was concerned about how she would feel when I would have to describe what she had done and the fact that she was indeed a murderer. Those are very harsh words. However, she told me that she understood and that was an indisputable part of her life. So, my reply to Janice was that I felt as if it were not my place to judge her and that she only had one final judge to face in the end.

As I spent time with Janice, I learned there were many different facets to her. The first thing was that she liked to be called Jan, hence the title to the book. Occasionally the 17-year-old girl would slip into the conversation and talk about teenager things such as having never been to Walmart or her fascination with electronics. Other times, I would see the woman who had loved the first man whom she deemed her knight in shining armor and then endured his beating her on her wedding night. Also, she admitted to the stark reality of waking up one day and realizing that he never loved her at all. Then there were times, when I saw the woman who was deeply remorseful for what she had done in her youth. She would talk about wishing she could go back and undo the terrible things she had done. Finally, I saw the woman who told me how she had taken another person's life and the toll that life behind bars had taken.

I never imagined myself entering a women's prison to sit beside Jan and talk about her life. When I finally met her face to face, I saw the stark reality of what thirty-six years behind bars can do to a person. The first thing she asked for was a hug, a simple sign of human compassion. I obliged and I think that simple show of trust allowed her the confidence to confide in me. I later found out that day that I was the first visitor, other than her attorney, that she had received in over ten years.

People have asked me what I think about life for Jan outside of prison walls. I have to simply say I don't know. That outcome will be left up to the authorities and of course, her. While trying my best to be neutral in presenting this information, I have diligently tried to give the reader a complete view of everything I have seen. I have included Jan's own thoughts and the thoughts of others that I felt added to the story.

Please look at this story with an open mind. I hope people will realize that at any given moment in our lives, we are all just one bad choice from being ripped away from all we hold dear.

Thank you, Jan, for entrusting me to be a witness to your life.

Introduction

This book is based on a crime that occurred in Dalton, Georgia, on September 3, 1980, at the Country Boy Inn. This horrendous act resulted in the untimely death of a young woman named Demetra Faye Parker. I had heard about this case when I was growing up, but it wasn't until I had published my first book that a dear friend asked me if I had any ideas for the next book. She shared with me the name of Janice Buttrum, the youngest woman sentenced to the electric chair in Georgia, and one of the perpetrators of the murder of Demetra Parker.

I read through over three thousand pages of documents regarding the multiple trials of both Janice Buttrum and her husband Danny. I also wrote a letter to Janice, who is currently serving multiple life sentences without the possibility of parole. Much to my surprise, Janice responded to my letter and a pen pal relationship began. Initially, I was concerned that I would be labeled as someone who enjoyed writing about women who were sentenced to the electric chair. With my first book regarding Eula Elrod's story, I wrote based on court transcripts, newspaper and magazine articles and family recollections. On the other hand, Janice is still living and has spent the last thirty-six years behind bars.

As I began conducting interviews with some of the key players involved in Janice's case, I was a little disconcerted that each of these individuals considered Janice the mastermind of the husband/wife duo. I thought to myself, "How could a 17-year-old manipulate her 28 year old abusive husband to do her bidding?" I was also struggling with the aspect of making sure that I was keeping a neutral perspective on presenting Janice's story. It finally dawned on me what my problem was.

We all look at things with a certain set of eyes, whether you call them "rose colored glasses" or not. I was looking at Janice from a mommy/teacher perspective. I am only four years younger than Janice. Was I was seeing Janice as the young girl born to a prostitute mother, who sold her child to a set of parents, who even though they loved her, had substance abuse problems of their own? This, in turn, led to a string of life events, including molestation, bullying, and eventually marriage to an abusive spouse at the tender age of fifteen. Naturally, my first impulse was to be sympathetic. I wanted to give her a hug and almost apologize for all that had seemed to go wrong in her life. Not long after that, the vision changed.

First, I had to look at the other people who were involved in Janice being sentenced to the electric chair. Her defense attorneys were upstanding men in the community. They had taken the tools that they had at hand and represented both Danny and Janice to the best of their ability, often times falling under the judgmental eyes of their friends and neighbors. For many, these cases would be some of the first of many landmark cases they would cover in their careers. I had to realize we did not have the benefits of DNA testing or even the luxury of calling 911 at the time. This was a 36-year-old case, and many of the modern conveniences we have available now certainly did not exist then. Even though I contacted many people regarding their roles in this case, some understandably chose not to participate. I can appreciate their desire to distance themselves from such a graphic crime, and I chose to respect that decision.

On September 10, 2016, I found myself in the visiting room in a women's prison. After several months of corresponding with Janice, and a couple of hiccups, I was granted the opportunity to visit Janice and sit across from her. I wondered what I was getting myself into. I looked around at the families around me waiting for their loved one to appear. In the meantime, thoughts were racing through my head. "What would she say? Would she even show? Did I really want to hear what she might tell me?"

There was a forty-five minute delay due to some other activities going on at the prison that day. When Janice walked in, she walked by me, waved and smiled, and then checked in with the prison guard. She then walked up to me and said "I am a hugger. Do you mind if I give you a hug?" This was the first of many times that I was at a loss of words, and people who know me can attest that is a rare occasion. About twenty minutes into our visit, she said to me, "I think we have walked around the elephant in the room long enough; I am ready to talk." It was those words that forever changed the way I saw this case.

Janice proceeded to tell me the story of how she met Demetra Faye Parker and then led me to the point where she administered the first stab wound. Indisputably, this first stab wound eventually became 90+ more that would end Demetra's life. I felt as if I had been punched in the stomach and couldn't breathe. It was then I realized I was sitting across from a murderer.

The following events are compiled from court transcripts, newspaper articles, personal interviews, and excerpts from Janice's personal journal. I have tried my best to portray all parties as equal participants. It is up to the reader to decide who orchestrated the final event. The one thing we can't forget is that Demetra Parker lost her life that night and justice must be served.

Chapter 1

During September in Georgia, the days are hot and muggy, the nights are still long, and the summer is winding to an end. People are leaving their doors open to enjoy the daylight a little longer, but little did one young woman know that monsters were on the other side of that door.

The Country Boy Inn was located just off Interstate 75 in the small community of Carbondale. The hotel was a place that catered to a transient population, people who were looking for a place to crash for a night or two. There was a truck stop nearby and a café where the weary traveler could pick up a greasy burger and a hot cup of coffee. This place was the temporary home of a young lady named Demetra Parker.

Demetra was a native of Kenton, Tennessee, who was just beginning to spread her wings, and she had followed her heart to Dalton, Georgia. Demetra had only been living in Dalton a month and was dating Henry Wallace, a young man from her hometown whom she had known for four years. Henry and Demetra had previously been living with Henry's brother and sister-in-law, but Demetra had needed some space and had been staying at the Country Boy Inn for about a week. She had been working in a local carpet mill, but unfortunately she had lost her job and had decided to make some changes. It was a new month, a new beginning, and Demetra was looking to make a fresh start of her life. She had ultimately decided to leave the hotel and move back in with her boyfriend, however, the next twenty-four hours would be life altering.

Tuesday, September 2nd, was the day after the long Labor Day weekend. Demetra was catching up on the small chores she had put off over the weekend. She was packing her car and happily planning for the future. Demetra had just met Janice Buttrum, a young mother residing at the hotel. Janice was not alone; she was there with her husband Danny and her 18-month-old daughter Alexis*. The young family had only been there a few days, and Danny was employed at the nearby truck stop doing minor mechanic duties. Demetra and Janice had not previously spent time together but that particular morning, they had been at the laundry mat together. Just being a sweet friend, Demetra had been showing Janice and Danny around the town and driving them to various spots.

After spending the morning together, Janice and Demetra parted ways at the hotel. Later in the evening Demetra called two friends, Donald Goforth and Timmy Sexton. She knew Timmy from working at Southern Binders, a local carpet mill, and he had introduced her to Donald. Demetra had spent most of the afternoon packing her car and was looking to spend some time winding down before she finished packing the following morning. She picked up the pair, and they returned to the Country Boy Inn to hang out. The trio was sitting in Demetra's hotel room with the door propped open. They had been watching the news and "The Rookies," a weekly TV police drama, when Demetra abruptly asked Donald to shut the door. In the estimated two and half hours the trio had been in Demetra's room, Danny Buttrum had been pacing back and forth in front of her door approximately fifteen to twenty times. Demetra stated that Danny gave her the "creeps" and told her friends that Danny had been paying unwanted attention to her

* Name changed to protect the innocent.

lately and it was making her uncomfortable and scared. The group stayed until "The Rookies" was over and decided to spend time somewhere else. Demetra ended up at her boyfriend's home, and Henry and she spent time together from 10 p.m. to about midnight.

Later, Demetra Parker was in her room trying to sleep. She had a lot on her mind. Things hadn't worked out quite as she had planned and she was regrouping. She had told Mr. Patel, the owner of the Country Boy Inn that she was leaving the hotel and would be by sometime the morning of September 3rd to turn in her keys. Around 4 a.m. she was awakened by a knock at her door.

Demetra got up off the bed and went to the door. She opened it just a crack and there was Janice, her neighbor from two doors down. Janice was standing there in the darkness and asked Demetra for a cigarette. She gave the excuse that the vending machine was out, and Danny was really wanting a cigarette. At first, Demetra protested the time of night and tried to deter her uninvited guest. After a couple of pleas from Janice, Demetra reached behind the door to retrieve a cigarette from the nearby table. As she turned away from the door, Danny Buttrum pushed his way into the room and shoved Janice out onto the balcony.

Court documents claim that Janice was on the other side of the door briefly but then willingly made the decision to enter the room belonging to Demetra Parker. Janice walked into the room holding her 18-month-old daughter in her arms. She picked up the phone off the bedside table and handed it to her daughter to occupy her. She sat her daughter on the carpet beside the side of the bed that was nearest the door. The next few moments and the choices she made would change

Janice's life forever. She rounded the corner of the bed and found her husband sexually assaulting Demetra. According to Janice, she picked up a knife off the bed and stabbed Demetra in the chest.

Very quickly the situation escalated to a frenzy. Both Danny and Janice began attacking Demetra. The couple stabbed her over and over. The next few minutes passed in a whirlwind of blood and gore and when the room stopped spinning Demetra was dead, lying in a pool of her own blood. It seemed there wasn't a space on Demetra's chest and abdomen that was not covered with stab wounds. Over ninety wounds were present by the time the carnage was done. The final blow came when Danny picked up the pocket knife and slashed Demetra across the lower abdomen leaving a gaping wound. Janice left the room with Alexis in her arms and Danny turned to try to wash away the blood. While he was scrubbing his hands, he noticed a yellow plastic toothbrush holder lying next to the sink. He thought the object was a device used for sexual pleasure. Danny turned once more to Demetra sprawled on the floor. In one final flourish of deviance and depravity, he shoved the object into Demetra's vagina.

An autopsy report would later reveal that there were 91 individual stab wounds. Sixty-seven stab wounds were located on the left anterior chest causing penetration of the left lung. There were twenty-four stab wounds to the throat and signs of possible manual strangulation. Signs of bruising were found on the right scalp, at the base of the nose/top of the lip, and the right jaw. The examination also revealed evidence of vaginal penetration but no semen was found.

No one will ever know for sure what happened in that hotel room. Three adults and one child were present in the room that night. We do know that one adult was left dead on the floor, and neither perpetrator testified in his/her own defense at the individual trials that followed. Worst of all, one small child had not yet gained her voice to communicate the horrid images her eyes had seen.

Part I
Home Sweet Home

Chapter 2

In order to better understand how something occurred, one has to understand the people and the series of life events that led up to a certain moment in time. So true with the story of Janice Buttrum. To better understand what led her to that bedside and put a knife in her hand, perhaps one must learn about Janice's earlier years.

The following is an excerpt from a journal containing memories written by Janice. This is how she described coming into this world.

> "January 17, 1963 – At 2:10 a.m. a baby girl was born to an 18-year-old mother. Marie Christian Beavers had been there before. Her first baby Jennifer lived just 18 months. She'd decided that she couldn't bear to keep another baby. For the last 8 months, she'd lived with the couple who would raise this little girl. When the nurse handed the baby to her new mother and asked for a name, no one had any ideas. They all had thought it would be a boy.
>
> The nurse was asked for her ideas. She was a Janis Joplin fan and suggested Janis and the birth Mother's first name. So that is how Janice Marie Beavers came into the world.
>
> Three days later when it was time to pick up the baby the snow was so deep that the only vehicle heavy enough to stay on the roads was the hearse from Barton's Funeral Home. Signs of things to come in

baby Janice's life."

There are however, conflicting reports to the early beginnings of Janice's life. Her mother was a prostitute and her biological father was unknown. Janice was the second of eight children born to Marie Beavers. Her mother struggled with drug addiction and her inability to care for her children so she chose her lifestyle over her children. It was reported that Janice was sold for sixty dollars to the couple who had paid her mother's outstanding hospital bill. This grieving couple had lost a child of their own, and they were looking for a child to fill the void. Mr. Barton of Barton's Funeral Home shared with them that he knew of a baby that was available. Although Ralph and Elizabeth Adcock never formally adopted Janice, they became her parents. Janice referred to herself as a black market baby.

The Adcocks were considerably older parents. Ralph, 51, was employed by the Department of Transportation and worked on the roads while Elizabeth, 42, was a housewife. They were simple people, but they too suffered from their own addictions. Both Ralph and Elizabeth drank alcohol excessively. According to family, Ralph was a gentle soul. He took care of Janice in the evenings when he got home from work and she was his buddy on Saturday when he took care of his various weekend errands. He was always looking out for the other children in the family as well. Ralph was forever finding bicycles and toys in the area landfill and eventually cleaned them up to give them to his nieces, nephews, and Janice to enjoy.

When Janice was four-years-old, her life started changing. Janice and her family's living conditions were altered. The family found themselves living in a three-room house consisting of a living room, bedroom, and kitchen. Janice described what her life was like in these surroundings:

> "I learned about committing to something and never turning back. I also learned how to avoid things like telling the truth if it hurt someone. I learned how to avoid acknowledging alcoholism, abuse, and hygiene wasn't taught. Sex wasn't discussed. God wasn't obeyed. My parents showed no affection for each other."

Even as a young child, Janice seemed not to follow the norm. She related the story of befriending a young black boy in her class, and they quickly became young "partners in crime." They were first caught stealing lunch money from their fellow classmates. Then, she claimed the pair once rain away from the school building but were quickly caught. Hoping to deter their rebellious behavior, teachers separated Janice and her new friend into different classrooms, but this only seemed to add to their mischief.

It was also during this time, that Janice began to experience bullying from her peers. During her competency trial, former teachers described what Janice was like during this awkward time in her life. Mary Caruthers taught Janice in the fourth grade and described her as a loner. She stated that Janice was unkempt and smelled, and her peers taunted her because of this. Ms. Caruthers believed that the role of the parent should include personal hygiene, morality, honesty, self-discipline and self-control. She did not feel that the Adcocks were meeting these basic needs for Janice.

Another teacher, Rose Johnson, who was Janice's fifth grade teacher, stated that Janice was an outsider. She also described Janice as a deprived child who was isolated by her peers. It is interesting to note that in Janice's memories, she stated that she thought the teachers encouraged the other children to pick on her. She saw herself as clean but not necessarily having new clothes. Throughout her life, her memories seem to reflect Janice seeing herself as a victim and that the things which happened to her occurred because of other's choices, not her own.

The summer after Janice's second grade year, Elizabeth Adcock entered Talmadge Hospital in Augusta to spend the summer being treated for a skin condition. It is unsure what kind of condition would necessitate a three-month stay in the hospital. However, Janice related the story that she was left in the care of a neighbor and the neighbor was incapable of taking care of her basic needs. She stated in her journal that the neighbor fed her only once a day and that this meal usually consisted of a hot dog, a bun and a glass of water. She claimed that this arrangement continued on for approximately two weeks until her father came to pick her up and found her outside under a tree crying because she was hungry. Her father quickly removed her from the situation after a verbal altercation with the caregiver. Mr. Adcock took her home, fed her a bowl of beef stew with a slice of loaf bread, and then attempted to bathe her and clean her long, unruly hair.

According to Janice's journal, she wrote that she was then taken to relative's house who had eight children and this was where she was left for the summer. It is unsure as to whether this was the same relative as above because the details are quite ambiguous. Janice stated that she struggled with playing well with others since she was used to being an only child. She related two different episodes where she struck out physically against her cousins. One of them was a male cousin who struck her because she refused to share a toy, and she stated that she picked up an item the equivalent of a toy bat and struck the young man. She was spanked for the outburst.

The second event involved a female cousin with whom she was spending the night. Janice claimed that during the night she needed to get up to go to the bathroom, and the cousin would not move out of her way. She stated that she deliberately stepped on the cousin's stomach as she exited the bed. This resulted in another spanking for Janice.

At the end of that eventful summer, Elizabeth returned from the hospital. Janice was also beginning the third grade. She related one more incident that occurred which showed Janice's developing violent tendencies. Janice described accompanying her father to the local laundry mat as one part of their Saturday routine. While at the laundry mat another little girl came up to Janice and began taunting her about Janice having a "crazy" mother. Janice said that she remembered pushing the young girl down and hitting her, but after that she couldn't remember anything else. It was at that point that her father rounded the corner and found Janice hitting the young girl's head against the concrete lip under the washer. He quickly pulled Janice off the young girl. In her journal, Janice stated, "That was the start of my rage against people who tell lies on or try to hurt people that I care about".

Janice did not share anything of significance of her third grade year other than she was accused of stealing five dollars from the teacher's desk. Again, she claimed that she had learned her lesson since her previous theft accusation in first grade and that the adults were just looking for someone to blame. Her one fond memory was of attending church with an older female cousin. She talked of enjoying the small church in the Folsom community and that she even got a Bible for perfect attendance.

It was the summer after third grade that Janice experienced a terrible tragedy. Janice shared that during this summer her biological mother reappeared in her life and that she ultimately learned that the Adcocks were not her real parents. She wrote about spending a wonderful summer's day getting newly acquainted with two of her sisters. However, she never got to go back to visit again. Janice stated she was unsure if this was due to Elizabeth's jealousy of her birth mother Marie or of the fear that Marie might take Janice away. Marie Beavers died shortly thereafter of cervical cancer at the age of twenty-nine. Janice stated that she left behind three to seven children. Jennifer, the oldest sister, died before Janice was born, and Janice recounted meeting two other half sisters, Carol and Donna. Janice said there were rumors of a half-brother and also a set of twins. She described her mother as being pretty and wanting to have fun.

At about this same time period, Janice described an incident where she was savagely attacked by a dog while her father was at work. Mrs. Adcock managed to stop the bleeding but did not seek medical attention until after Mr. Adcock got home. A relative confirmed this story and stated that Janice came to her home and that she had been bitten on her crown by a dog. The woman stated that Janice's hair was matted from the blood as well as from being neglected. She washed Janice's hair multiple times but at some point told Mr. Adcock that she would have to cut Janice's hair in order to repair the damage. He conceded to allow Janice's hair to be cut but Mrs. Adcock was upset about her baby losing her curls. This relative also related that she took Janice down to a nearby creek to play in the water during the summer with her own children. During these excursions, the relative would take soap and towels and combine bathing with playing.

One last fond memory of Janice's early childhood was of her fourth grade teacher, Mary Caruthers. She described Mary as one of the best teachers she ever had. She stated that this teacher encouraged her to use her brain and was also the only teacher who, up until that point had made any effort to meet Janice's parents. Janice expressed a sense of pride at excelling at spelling and Georgia History. It was at this point that Janice's memories blended together for the next few years, but things would quickly turn tragic in Janice's life once again.

Chapter 3

When people watch the popular crime shows on TV, the profilers frequently describe the unsub as suffering some type of catastrophic event in his/her life that starts life on a downward spiral. With Janice, these life changing events started occurring when she became a teenager.

At this time, Janice related that she probably lost the one girl that she saw as her best friend. She stated that she knew Judy Long from her daily bus ride. Although, Judy was sixteen and three years older than Janice, they spent their daily commute sharing the normal secrets that young girls do. One day Judy confided in Janice that she was quitting school because her father was forcing her to get married. Janice was heartbroken and wondered which one of them had a worse life.

The most devastating event occurred shortly thereafter. The man that Janice considered her hero, her father, died. Janice's described it as a brief illness, where he was hospitalized at a local hospital and then moved to a VA hospital. Another relative described the illness as being very aggressive. By the time Mr. Adcock sought treatment for his illness, it was too late. All Janice knew was that the man who represented normalcy in her life was gone.

Janice described the relationship with her mother as rocky. Mrs. Adcock was quick to point out to Janice that her birth mother was a prostitute and that Janice would more than likely follow in her footsteps. Social workers remarked that Mrs. Adcock often stated that she had "paid" for Janice and could say whatever she wanted. Carol Rose, who was the public health nurse in Bartow County, stated she had known Janice since she was five. She visited Janice approximately four times a year until 1979. During Janice's competency trial, Ms. Rose testified that after Mr. Adcock passed away, Janice's living conditions abruptly changed. She stated that after his passing, Mrs. Adcock usually required a day's notice before one of Ms. Rose's visit. She often felt that would provide sufficient time for Mrs. Adcock to get sober.

A mere nine weeks after Mr. Adcock's death, Mrs. Adcock brought another man, Harold Peace, into the home. Mrs. Adcock described this man as being a former friend of her late husband. Janice said she knew that her mother was lying. She had always been her father's weekend companion while running errands around town and she had met all of her father's friends. Harold Peace was definitely not one of them.

Shortly after Harold moved in, he made the claim that he was Janice's biological father, although this was never proven. Mrs. Adcock told Janice that she needed to be nice to Mr. Peace. In her journal, Janice described one incident shortly after Harold's arrival. This would broaden the crack in the relationship between Janice and her mother. One Saturday, Harold took Janice to the liquor store with him. This was a weekly ritual that she'd had with her dad. Her father would purchase liquor for himself and Elizabeth and purchase Sprite for Janice. Harold was trying to follow the same routine. Janice said that she thanked Harold for the Sprite and went back to reading the book that she had brought with her. Later that night after Mrs. Adcock had gone to bed, Harold showed up at Janice's bedside seeking more gratitude. According to Janice, he attempted to fondle her and then kiss her. She screamed at the top of her lungs, which was enough to wake her mom and scare him off. He left but not without whispering to her, "This isn't over."

Janice said she waited until she thought everyone was asleep and took a few of her possessions, and went to a paternal cousin's house close by. From there she contacted Carol Rose, the county nurse, and after that, the Department of Family and Children's Services. The following Monday, Janice found herself in the foster care system. Her first placement was with a family by the name of Brown in Dallas, Georgia. She described the couple as having a grown daughter, a 17-year-old son, and a daughter younger than Janice.

Janice described the foster system experience as the DEFACS episode. She noted that she had to follow real rules. Janice said that she felt out of place, and she acknowledged this was when she began to feel afraid of change. Her analogy was being on the outside of a bubble looking in to it. Janice did have some good experiences, such as getting new clothes that were just for her, records for her personal record player, and trying new things like eating homemade spaghetti. However, this did not last long because the foster care system decided to put Janice up for adoption since she did not legally belong to Elizabeth Adcock.

For Janice the first year of her teenage years was quite tumultuous. She described being in and out of a series of foster homes. Each time, it seemed as if Janice was too rebellious to settle into a normal family. One particular episode stood out in which Janice acted out in rage but could not remember exactly what she had done. She was staying in a foster home when another child was brought into the home. He was five-years-old and had been the victim of physical abuse. The young boy was left in Janice's care, and she described falling asleep one night while comforting the crying boy. She claimed that she missed the school bus the next morning, and the foster mother became irate with her. According to Janice, the woman was yelling at her and that Janice reciprocated by calling her a foul name. The woman supposedly struck her in anger and Janice struck back. She claimed that no one wanted to believe her story.

Janice also described another foster home where she was folding clothes and the woman was belittling her. Janice grabbed a coat hanger off the dresser and threw it on the floor. However, she claimed that the woman told DEFACS that Janice struck her with the hanger. Obviously, Janice saw herself as the victim in these situations. It was always the system that was responsible for putting her in the very center of these volatile episodes.

Finally, Janice was placed in the Murphy Harpst Home in Cedartown. This place was described as a residential treatment facility that aids children who have been viciously abused. They prided themselves on being able to help children re-engage with society and lead productive lives. Janice described the place as a dorm-like environment with little supervision. Again, she described another episode of striking another human being in a fit of rage because a boy she supposedly had an interest in was kissing another girl.

Left with no other options, DEFACS decided to return Janice to the home of Elizabeth Adcock with the promise that if Harold tried to bother her again that they would come to her rescue. She was returned in December, 1976, and described Harold taking her and her mother to Florida to visit his family over the holidays. She had a good time at the beach and loved the ocean.

Chapter 4

When Janice returned home from Florida, she found that the place she called home didn't exist anymore. Janice claimed that Harold had encouraged Elizabeth to sell her house and land. They were now living in a pull camper which consisted of a bedroom, a bathroom and a living/kitchen area. Janice found herself sleeping on the couch, but she soon exercised her independence and moved into an abandoned van in the backyard.

With the New Year came new changes. Janice admitted that with turning fourteen she decided she could do what she wanted. School became a trivial point in her life. She said up to that time, she had done well in school but began to struggle once she reached this level. It was because of her sporadic school attendance that she came under the radar of Marvin Dickerson, a school social worker for the Bartow County Board of Education.

Just a few years later, Marvin would be called to testify during Janice's sentencing phase. He was the Truancy Officer when he first encountered Janice and saw firsthand her horrendous living conditions. He tried to make home visits with Mrs. Adcock, but she would say that Janice was not there. Their primary residence was an 8 x 35 foot long trailer. There was an old van with no wheels that was resting on concrete blocks in the back yard.

Marvin went on to describe Mrs. Adcock and her addiction to alcohol. He stated that every time he saw Mrs. Adcock that she was under the influence of alcohol. The only time he ever saw her sober was on those occasions when he was forced to take her to court. He described Janice as being a very kind child, who showed kindness when she was treated with kindness.

There was one occasion that Marvin related that showed just how emotionally abusive Elizabeth could be to Janice. They were in the courthouse awaiting their turn to appear. Marvin was standing next to the duo when he overheard Mrs. Adcock say to Janice, "I hate you and I hope I never see you again." Marvin said the look on Janice's face was that of someone having a bucket of cold water thrown in her face. Janice replied, "Well, I hate you too."

Janice quit school at the age of fourteen during her 7th grade year. She began trying to find a place to fit in and call home. Janice described in her journal that during this time she was once again taken into the custody of DEFAC. She was sent to live with a former caseworker and for a brief time period, Janice experienced being part of a family unit. The mother wanted to formalize this arrangement and make Janice a part of the family, but the case worker was against it. Her husband had gotten a job transfer to Arizona and wanted the entire family unit to move there. The mother wanted to stay in Georgia until the school year ended and the papers came through to make Janice a permanent part of their home. However, after a brutal argument, the father prevailed.

The next day, Janice told the couple she was going to visit her mother. She arrived to find both Elizabeth and Harold inebriated. It was at this moment that Janice felt her life situation needed to change. She called Billy, a boy she considered a boyfriend. Janice decided that she had to find a way to support herself, and her plan consisted of following in the footsteps of her mother. Janice felt that she could support herself by working in the world's oldest profession although at this point in her life, she was still a virgin. She offered Billy this prized possession in exchange for a one-way drive to Atlanta. Billy did not have a car but told Janice that he had a friend who would provide transportation for the pair.

Janice described the events of that fateful trip. The trio stopped at Allatoona Dam so that she could fulfill her promise to Billy. The friend got out of the car in order to give the pair some privacy. She said that Billy was gentle with her but there were no fireworks. He got out of the car and left Janice to get dressed. As soon as Billy got out of the car, his friend got in and raped Janice. She struggled against his advances, but he was very aggressive. Janice attempted to run away once the attack was over. Billy caught up with her and apologized for his friend's unwanted advances. The trio rode around for the rest of the evening, even picking up another female for Billy's friend.

Even though she didn't make it to Atlanta that day, Billy took her home with him and stated that he would give her a temporary place to live. Billy's mother was very upset about the new visitor in her home. After a loud argument between Billy and his mother, the mother called the police on Janice. Janice left the home and after walking for a brief stint, she was picked up by the police and taken to jail.

The police tried to get her to file statutory rape charges against Billy but Janice refused. She never mentioned Billy's friend who had raped her. This was something that she would not acknowledge until much later. She was taken to the Regional Youth Developmental Center (RYDC) in Rome until they could decide what to do with her. Janice related that at some point she believed the judge was going to give her the opportunity to return to Elizabeth Adcock. However, Elizabeth said that she didn't want Janice anymore. She stated that she wasn't legally hers and that she couldn't control Janice anymore.

It was finally decided that Janice would go to the main female facility for the Youth Developmental Center that was located in Macon. She described the facility almost as if she were describing a college campus. The girls each had their own individual area which included a bed, a closet, a desk with drawers, and a chair. They had washers and dryers and were given money each week on their commissary account. The inhabitants of the facility were also able to cook their own meals on the weekend. Janice also depicted the center as having a TV area as well as a huge stereo.

Janice seemed happy at YDC. She revealed that the facility also offered a trade/vocation program. Through this program, Janice learned such things as how to run a cash register, sew her own clothes and how to type. One of her favorite activities that she participated in was choir. The group she was in was allowed to go to churches and nursing homes to perform. The one thing that she liked the best was attending a real summer camp. Janice was only supposed to be at the facility three months but she decided to attempt an escape. She said the futile attempt lasted a mere nine hours before she and her accomplice turned themselves in to the authorities. The reason for this was that her cohort in crime wouldn't stop whining.

Janice was given a psychiatric evaluation in October, 1977, as a result of being a part of the state system. In the doctor's notes, he wrote that initially Janice did not like the group setting because she thought the others in the home were against her. She had attempted to run away and was put in isolation for five days. Janice stated that she did realize that she needed to work on problems so that she could become a good candidate to continue in the group home setting.

Janice was asked to describe her past home life situation. She confessed that her mother drank on almost a daily basis and that sometimes she did strike her. She stated that her father was very nice. She did mention the fact that he drank as well, but that he disciplined her only when it was necessary. Her opinion of her stepfather was completely opposite. He was described as a drinker, and one who made unwanted advances toward Janice. However, in spite of all this, she did express the desire to go back and live with her mother. The examiner stated that he thought Janice would be an ideal candidate for a group home, but he doubted that she would ever be suitable for a foster home. He also said that she was hungry for affection. His notes also indicated that Janice was a compliant person and her impulsivity and poor judgment make her vulnerable to the suggestions of other, stronger personalities. The examiner also predicted that she would also tolerate long periods of abuse before she developed enough aggressive energy to escape. Janice was given a clinical diagnosis of runaway reaction of adolescence and immature personality.

Not long after this, Janice was accepted into the Georgia Industrial Home in Macon. This was in 1977, and Janice remembered this because it was the fall after Elvis Presley had passed away. Each girl was sponsored by a family and Janice was allowed to meet hers around Christmas of that year. The family took her to see the Nutcracker and gave her a serape as a gift. Janice was enrolled at Miller B. Junior High in Bibb County and was again able to take choir as an elective. She enjoyed a sense of normalcy for a while but that was short-lived. Janice once again tried to find freedom from her confinement. When she was recaptured and sent back to the center, she confessed to the director that she was ready to return home to Elizabeth.

Janice returned to the YDC in Rome and had to appear in Juvenile Court in Cartersville. Elizabeth Adcock showed up to this hearing and admitted to the judge that she was ready for Janice to return home. In Janice's words, "Finally after fifteen years of not being her child, she was awarded legal custody of me." When Janice returned to the home, she found there was no alcohol and no boyfriend, and for a short period of time, the young lady and her mother were friends again. Elizabeth decided the pair needed a fresh start and returned home to Adairsville. They parked their travel trailer behind a gas station that was owned by a friend of Mr. Adcock's. Janice then described what happened next, "This is where we lived when I met the man who totally changed the rest of my life."

PART II
Janice Loves Danny

Chapter 5

Falling in love for the first time is something most teenage girls can't forget. She can describe in detail that moment in time when she finds the man who captures her heart. Her eyes light up and she has that special smile on her face. The same can be said for Janice as she describes the first time that she "laid eyes on Danny Buttrum." The date was May 11, 1978, Mother's Day. Janice describes that moment in time. Danny was twenty-six and she was fifteen.

> "He was one of the prettiest boys, I had ever seen. He was a little taller than me and had curly brown hair and big brown eyes. He dressed nicely and was so polite to my Mama. He said Ma'am and Sir. Most boys didn't do that in the 70's. His name was Danny. I always told Mama that he was her Mother's Day present. I loved him from the time I saw him and God help me, I love him still."

Janice has now said that she was not in love with him, but "with the person he was when he was really himself." She stated that Danny was never really diagnosed with anything by a professional, but he was not the same man the last seven to eight months that they spent together.

Janice described the day as a whirlwind. The couple drove around together and made a stop at a convenience store for cigarettes. They had spent the day laughing and talking. She described the perfect moment, "I grabbed him and I French kissed him. He smiled and had my heart from that moment onward."

As the day progressed, the group became stranded due to car trouble. Danny and Janice had to hitchhike back to Elizabeth's house. In that time together, they talked about what all young people in love do. The couple talked about babies, getting married, and growing old together. When they got back to Elizabeth and the others, Elizabeth asked them when they were getting married. Danny said, "Tomorrow." The pair ended up spending the night together. Janice said the two had attempted to consummate their relationship but were unable to complete the act. Danny claimed that had never happened to him before despite his drunken state. The two were unable to get married the next day, because Danny did not have a birth certificate since he had been born at home.

For the next three weeks, the couple played a game of cat and mouse trying to hide from both of their probation officers. They divided their time between Janice's house and Danny's house. The two soon slipped up and were caught by Janice's probation officer at her home. The probation officer decided to arrange a meeting with Danny's probation officer, Elizabeth, Danny, and Janice.

At the meeting, the pair was given three options. The first option was for them to get married. It is unsure whose initial idea it was that a grown man of twenty-six should be getting married to an underage young girl. The second option was for the couple to go their separate ways and not have any contact with each other. However, the flip side to their decision was that if they stayed together, they would have the option of having their respective probations revoked. This would result in Danny being sent to a work camp and Janice going back to YDC. Looking at the total picture, it seemed like a no-win situation for all parties involved. There was one aspect of the equation that no one was considering. Young Janice was pregnant.

Danny had been married previously to a young woman named Candy. This union had produced a young son but the marriage had been a tumultuous one. Later on a picture of violence would emerge involving the young couple and the two would part ways. It had been a difficult divorce with Candy not allowing Danny to see their child. One can only imagine the stories Danny had told to garner sympathy from Janice. One thing was for sure, Janice did not want to keep the baby she was expecting away from Danny.

Janice was faced with some very tough choices for a fifteen-year-old girl to make. Here was someone who had never had a permanent home of her home. A product of a system that had failed her, she wanted someone to love her and that she could love in return. Janice knew that if she was returned to YDC that the child she was carrying would be put up for adoption. What feelings and emotions that she must have been struggling with inside her own mind. Janice had reached a point in her life in which she was with someone who she thought loved her. Life had not dealt her the best hand, but she still grasped at what she saw as the ideal package.

Janice and Danny still decided to pursue getting married. Their first stop was the state of Alabama. They were turned away because again Danny needed a birth certificate. Their next stop was Calhoun, Georgia where they got a copy of Janice's birth certificate. The journey continued to Cartersville where they applied for a marriage license. The couple then had to go to a doctor so that Janice could get a document that showed proof of pregnancy. After all of this, Elizabeth then refused to sign for the couple to get married. However, since she was not Janice's birth mother or her legal guardian, the clerk gave the pair a license to get married.

Danny and Janice returned to Adairsville where they searched for the Justice of the Peace, Odell Adcock, who happened to be Janice's uncle. The couple were married at the Church of God, but Elizabeth refused to enter the church to watch the pair exchange their vows. There were no witnesses to this wedding on June 26, 1978. Janice equated the event to a country love song. However, just like the typical country ballad, there would be love and heartache involved. Janice said the night ended with bruises and a black eye because she didn't want Danny doing drugs on their wedding night. Janice had never mentioned if there had been any violence prior to this event. She only stated in her journal that this was not the first time that he had hurt her nor would it be the last.

Life for the newlyweds was a struggle. Danny got a job as a mechanic at a truck stop near the interstate. He worked three to four days in a row, then he was off for two. As Janice's pregnancy progressed, Danny wanted Janice to go to work with him. Janice would do his paperwork and write the receipts while Danny worked on vehicles. Janice described this as one of the good times they had. She said they had a steady income, never ran out of food and had lots of material things. Finally feeling love, Janice said Danny accepted her just the way she was. The honeymoon stage didn't last for long.

Janice remarked that the man that she loved and the man Danny would evolve into were not the same person. Janice's family was not accepting of Danny. She described meeting family members at social events and that none of them seemed to like Danny. They could never give a specific reason to Janice for this dislike but she felt ostracized. Her extended family members said that once the pair got married, they saw less and less of Janice. It might seem that the groom was very protective of his new bride. Looking back, it might be easier to see this as a classic example of an abuser, isolation from family and being possessive. Records later showed that Janice took out multiple warrants due to physical abuse, but like many victims, she would go back and withdraw the warrants.

The small little family of two would soon become three. The couple's daughter was born in February, 1979. Janice said that Danny stayed with her throughout the labor and delivery. She stated that it was the first time that she had ever seen him cry. From that moment, baby Alexis had her father wrapped around her little finger. Janice once remarked if Danny had lived, little Alexis would not have dated anyone before her 21st birthday.

For about three months after Alexis was born, Danny seemed like the ideal father. He was working regularly and coming home at night to spend time with baby Alexis. He would help feed, bathe and change the baby, and even helped Janice around the house.

Jealousy soon began to rear its ugly head. Janice described having to call a cab in order to go to the grocery store because the couple didn't have a car. There was an older cabbie who had befriended Janice. He would help Janice with her purchases, but most of all he treated her like an adult. He respected her and was probably just looking out for her like a father figure. Danny informed her in no uncertain terms that she needed to find a new cabbie.

On Mother's Day, 1979, Danny started acting out again. Janice felt she had shown him that she loved him. However, Danny had started hanging out with some rough guys at work and had started using drugs again. The couple went to Evelyn Buttrum's house, Danny's mom, every weekend. She seemed to be the one person who could control Danny's behavior. On this weekend, Danny was arrested for disorderly conduct. Evelyn and Janice went into town to retrieve Danny from jail. When they arrived at the jail, they found that Danny had stuck paper in the air conditioning unit and set the paper on fire. Evelyn managed to convince the police to let Danny go with the promise that he would not return to town on the weekends.

Danny it seems was quite the momma's boy. Since Danny was the youngest of Evelyn's four sons, he was quite possibly a momma's boy. He was characteristically known for being a trouble maker but mom always seemed to be able to come behind to smooth any ruffled feathers. Evelyn had even gone as far to become a bondswoman so she could bail Danny out of jail at a moment's notice. Nevertheless, Danny had several encounters with law enforcement over a period of a few months which resulted in his probation being revoked and he was sent to jail.

There was only one thing that stood between Danny and the possibility of his serving some major time and that was Janice. Evelyn did all she could to persuade her not to testify against her baby boy. Evelyn took Janice out shopping and even bought her make-up to cover the bruises that Danny left behind. The judge saw through this façade, and Danny was sentenced to six months in a work camp located in Marietta.

During this time, Janice moved back in with her mom in Adairsville. She signed up for food stamps and government assistance under Evelyn's guidance. Evelyn had stated to friends that she didn't want to be left taking care of a baby that might not even belong to Danny. Janice's independence soon led to some reckless behavior. She stated that she soon found herself sleeping during the day and roaming around at night with Alexis in tow. She also described becoming promiscuous and confessed, “I’m not proud of it but it filled a need inside me I can’t explain. I wanted to feel special and needed. I did for those brief encounters.”

Janice struggled with the living arrangement she had with her mother. Elizabeth was still drinking daily. Janice described one incident in which she left Alexis briefly with her mother while she went to the store for apple juice and baby aspirin. While Janice was gone, Elizabeth passed out and somehow left the front door of the trailer open. During this same time period, Evelyn arrived at the home to find Alexis attempting to climb her way out. Because of this episode, Janice decided to rent an efficiency apartment. She had only lived there for a short period before Danny returned home. Shortly thereafter, the landlord evicted them.

By the time the holidays rolled around, Danny, Janice, and Alexis found themselves homeless. Danny’s brother and sister-in-law provided them shelter in exchange for babysitting while they worked. Janice was confident that they had enough love to last through the good times and the bad times. Unfortunately, love didn’t pay the bills.

Danny and Janice then began a cycle of moving from place to place. Janice fondly remembered one trailer park because it was spring break. The kids in the trailer park befriended the teenage girl with a baby and were soon spending most of the day with them just hanging out. Danny was working on a city garbage truck while waiting to get his driver’s license back. It had been suspended because of repeated episodes of driving under the influence.

Looking back, Janice realized that she was dealing with an addict, and she was becoming his enabler. Every time Danny got into trouble with the law, Janice was quick to come to his rescue. It was always someone else's fault and poor Danny saw himself as being picked on by those in charge. It was never Danny's fault that his choices were getting him in trouble.

The Buttrum home quickly became a hotspot for visits from law enforcement. Danny's drug and alcohol use had escalated and he thought of himself as "ten feet tall and bulletproof." Janice described one evening in particular when police were called to their home because Danny had locked himself in the bathroom with Alexis and refused to come out. He threatened the police with a knife; however, they did not arrest him. Janice though had had enough. She left with Alexis and went to a battered women's shelter in Rome. Nevertheless, family was quick to coax her back home to Danny.

A family member related the story that there was one person whom Janice trusted the most. This woman was a cousin of her dad's, and she had taken Janice to church as a child. She was someone that Janice loved and that she sought out when life with Danny became too much. This family member stated that Janice once showed up at Grace's** door seeking refuge.

Finally having enough of Danny's abuse, Janice had reached the point where she was taking Alexis and running away. However, what she didn't realize was that Grace did not believe in divorce. Grace sat Janice down and explained to her how she felt. She was told that she had to go back to Danny and make her marriage work. Grace then told her she was going to be the one to take her back. She couldn't take her to the door, but she would drop her off in the driveway. Undeniably, Janice must have finally felt stark reality smacking her in the face. Most of all, accepting that this was coming

** Name changed to protect the innocent

from someone whom she trusted. Janice said during this time she could hear Elizabeth's voice taunting her in her head. "You made your bed, now you have to lay in it."

Finally, it came down to the proverbial straw that broke the camel's back. Danny was pulled over one final time for a DUI. He failed the breathalyzer test and became belligerent with the arresting officers. He demanded a blood test and even went as far as calling one of the officers a derogatory name. As always when not getting his way Danny became violent. During this tantrum, Janice was in the lobby with baby Alexis. She heard the commotion going on and once again she wanted to hurry to the aid of Danny. As she tried to approach the door, an officer stepped in to detain her. She handed Alexis to the dispatcher and again made an attempt to push her way past the officer. Even though this was a 6'3", 250 lb. officer, Janice was charged with assault. Janice pled guilty and was given one year of probation. Danny ultimately violated his probation and his final fourteen months of probation were revoked. He was again sentenced to a work camp.

Janice went to live in a trailer next door to Evelyn Buttrum. Danny called home twice a week. One phone call he would talk to his mother and the other he would talk to Janice. A short time later, deputies from the Bartow County Sheriff's office arrived at Evelyn's home with a warrant for Danny. Trying to laugh the situation off, Evelyn stated that Danny was already incarcerated. The deputies explained to her that the warrant was for Danny being a habitual violator. If Danny was found guilty this time, he could serve 8-25 years in prison. When the deputies left, Evelyn turned to Janice and told her not to tell Danny. Janice felt as if he had a right to know and their next phone call would only be the beginning of the storm that was starting to brew.

Part III
Country Boy Inn

Chapter 6

Many people have asked, how did Danny and Janice come to be at the Country Boy Inn? What brought them along the path to Demetra Parker?

Danny was unhappy being at the work camp. Maybe he had a chance to look into the future, and he didn't like what he saw. Whatever the case may be, Danny devised a plan to escape from the work camp. Different versions of the story show Janice as his accomplice, but others say it was friends of his. One fact was for sure, Danny was free and knew he couldn't go back to his family home where he would surely be caught. He soon found work with an old friend, John Teems, at the Phillips 66 truck stop at Carbondale. Maybe this spot off the beaten path would be a place the cops wouldn't come looking him.

After Danny's escape in July, 1980, Danny and Janice found themselves renting a room at the Country Boy Inn. The motel was a typical establishment that catered to a transient population. There were areas of the motel that were for the tired traveler looking for a place to lay his head for the night. On the backside of the hotel, there was another area designated for those who "lived" at the motel. They paid a reasonable weekly rate to call the motel home.

At first Danny and Janice came alone. Their daughter had been left with relatives while the couple got settled. Danny was working at the truck stop, and Janice was spending her days alone at the motel. They had no car and relied on the kindness of strangers for rides. Janice begged Danny to allow Alexis to come stay with her. She needed someone with her to pass the time and taking care of her baby was the perfect solution.

It didn't take Danny long to fall into his old habits. He was using a combination of over-the-counter speed washed down with enough alcohol to make it through the day. Days ran into nights, and nights ran into days. Unfortunately, it would not take long for this powder keg to explode. For the moment, he was flying under law enforcement's radar, but that would quickly come to an end.

A typical day at the motel consisted of the tenants doing their blue collar jobs if they had one. During their off time, one would find clusters of people hanging out with neighbors on the concrete ledges in front of their rooms. The motel had a pool and a few of the tenants would gather around there to hang out as well. It was a hand-to-mouth existence for most.

Demetra Parker was one of those tenants. She resided in Room 263, just two doors down from Danny and Janice. She was a brown-haired, brown-eyed beauty with a heart of gold. Love had brought Demetra to Dalton. However, she had been living at the Country Boy Inn after a break-up with her boyfriend. Demetra had quickly been drawn to Alexis, the 19-month-old daughter of the Danny and Janice. She always had a soft spot for babies and Alexis always seemed to have a sweet, welcoming smile on her face. Demetra had helpfully driven Danny and Janice around their small community. She had shown them where to get groceries, where to do their laundry, and just the typical things a friend does.

Janice described the fateful day that she met Demetra Parker. On September 2, 1980, Janice described walking down the road with a trash bag over one shoulder and trying to balance her baby in the other arm. Demetra stopped her car, rolled down the window and asked Janice where she was going. When she found she was headed to the laundry mat, too, she opened the passenger door and offered her a ride. They spent the morning washing clothes together. Janice said this was the best girlfriend time she had in a very long time. The girls talked and giggled about all the things teen girls talk about when they are together. Their time was short lived. Demetra was headed back to Kenton, Tennessee, the next day, and Janice would be headed back to her lonely life at the motel. The two young girls, along with baby Alexis, returned to the Country Boy Inn and parted ways. Less than twenty-four hours later, one of them would be dead at the hands of the other.

Danny had worked the weekend at the truck stop. He used "black beauties" to help him stay awake at work. When he got back to the motel across the street, he would spend his free time consuming alcohol. He had been taking "speed" since age twelve and became addicted to alcohol soon afterwards. Danny consumed alcohol on a daily basis, and it was fairly common for him to consume a quart of liquor a day and follow that with a six-pack of beer.

Danny was waiting for Janice when she returned to the hotel. He was hanging out on the ledge outside their room with his new-found friend, Leon Busby. Leon was also living at the Country Boy Inn, and the two had decided to celebrate their new friendship by drinking a beer together. Danny introduced Janice to Leon and the group decided to go riding around.

The quartet, Leon, Danny, Janice, and baby Alexis rode aimlessly around for a couple of hours. Their first stop was at the home of Sybil Rogers. Sybil lived at the Peach State Motel and worked at the Amoco Truck Stop at Connector 3.

She knew Danny from seeing him at the truck stop where she was a waitress but had never met Janice. She was at her home on the night of September 2nd with her boyfriend Herschel Thomason when Danny showed up around 11:30 p.m. and asked to speak to her in private, but Herschel would not let her. Sybil would later testify that she saw Leon Busby and a blonde-haired woman in the car. She stated that Danny did not appear drunk to her. One can probably surmise that her boyfriend likely saved her life that night.

Their next stop was at the apartment of Dorothy Chastain. She had just moved out of the Country Boy Inn the day before. This was the second time that day that Danny had been by her new place. The first time was between 6 and 7 p.m. and Dorothy later confirmed he had been drinking at the time. The second time was between 11:00 p.m. and midnight, and she noticed he was in Leon Busby's car. She had been heating some water on the stove prior to Danny coming by her place. Just as she answered the door, her kettle whistled. She walked away from the door to remove the kettle and when she turned around Danny was in her kitchen. He was behind her and started to reach for her. She quickly pushed his hands away and told him he would have to leave. Danny left the apartment without an argument. However, the whole episode was very upsetting to Dorothy, and decided to get dressed and go to the truck stop where she worked. She drove by her friend Sybil Roger's apartment on her way and noticed Leon Busby's car parked there. Dorothy later testified that she knew both Danny and Janice, since she had worked with Danny at the truck stop. Dorothy also stated that she had seen Danny drinking earlier in the evening. She had asked Danny to leave her apartment and not to return unless Janice was with him.

The trio returned to the hotel around 11 p.m., and Danny

asked Leon if he and Janice could take the car out alone and Leon conceded. The couple left in the car and drove to Adairsville and a few places before returning the car nearly four hours later. That was when things started going wrong.

Pam Henry was also a resident at the Country Boy Inn. She was staying on the back side of the hotel near the expressway, where most long-termers were living. She stated that during the early morning hours someone woke her up by beating on her door. She thought the time was around 3:00 a.m. She called the maintenance man who lived on the site and asked him to come check and see who was at her door. He told her it was probably a drunk or someone at the wrong door. She was too scared to open the door or push back the curtain to see who might be on the other side. That particular move probably saved her life. Around 4 a.m. she claimed to hear a woman's voice screaming, and the voice seemed to be coming from upstairs. She, unfortunately, did not call maintenance this time.

The following reflects Janice Buttrum's version of what transpired next. She claims that either by divine intervention or personal choice, her memory does not allow her to remember after the first stab wound. Some of the details that she gives do not match the calendar date's events. For instance, she states that she was watching the Jerry Lewis Labor Day Telethon, which would have occurred on Monday of that week. However, Demetra was murdered in the early hours of Wednesday morning.

According to Janice, she was watching TV and Danny was pacing the room like a caged animal. He kept repeating over and over, "I am gonna kill her, I am gonna kill her." He looked over at Janice and said he needed cigarettes. He convinced Janice to go to Demetra's door, two doors away and ask for cigarettes, or whatever ruse she could use to get Demetra to the door. Janice kept putting him off, saying she didn't want to go. After several minutes, Danny convinced her to do this for him. She reluctantly left their room and went to Demetra's where she knocked on the door and waited. After several minutes, Demetra spoke to her from the other side. Janice asked her for cigarettes, stating she didn't have change for the vending machine and could she bum a couple till morning. After initially putting her off, Demetra relented and handed her a couple of cigarettes.

When Janice returned to her room, Danny was still pacing the floor with the same intensity as before she left. Hesitantly, she handed him the cigarettes and waited. He spent the next minute or two wildly throwing objects around looking for a lighter but with no luck. For a second time, he turned to Janice and told her to return to Demetra's room to ask for matches. Janice tried to refuse, not wanting to return again for fear of what could happen to her or Demetra.

Janice again made the trek to Demetra's door and raised her hand to knock. Again Demetra's sleepy voice answered from the other side. Janice identified herself; this time making a request for matches. When Demetra answered the door this time, Janice gave her a hug and a kiss. At that precise moment, Janice claimed that an "object" shot out of the darkness and pushed its way into the room. In the process, she was shoved out onto the ledge, and the door was slammed closed in her face. It was at this moment, that she heard the screams of baby Alexis.

Walking the few steps to her room, Janice found the door standing ajar and baby Alexis sitting alone on the bed screaming. She picked her up to soothe her cries and simultaneously heard a woman's scream coming from the direction of Demetra's room. She walked back toward the direction of the screams and stood outside the door. So many thoughts were racing through her head. Should she take this chance and run? Should she go in and save Demetra from the monster inside? What tilted the scales to cause her next move?

Reaching for the doorknob, Janice entered Demetra's room. She placed Alexis on the floor and handed her the rotary phone to play with. Never once did she think of picking up that same phone and calling for help to stop the carnage unfolding in front of her. Her steps took her around the corner of the bed. It was there that her eyes took in the vision of Danny on top of Demetra. He was sexually assaulting her and in his eyes she could see that look of rage she had seen so many times before.

Without a thought of hesitation, Janice picked up a knife that was lying on the bed. She grasped the knife in her right hand and in one thrust, the knife made contact with Demetra's upper right chest just above her heart. It is then that Janice's memory faded to black. Court documents state that both Janice and Danny took turns stabbing Demetra. There was also bruising on her jaw indicating that she was struck by something or someone. Bruising on her neck showed that at some point Demetra had been manually strangled.

The attack was fueled by a combination of anger, jealousy, and pure rage. Danny and Janice attacked Demetra with a vengeance, both of them taking turns stabbing her. All the while, the couple's 19-month-old daughter Alexis crawled around the room. One resident reported a woman's scream but it is unknown how long Demetra survived after the first stab wound was inflicted. There are conflicting reports as to which one administered the large gaping wound across Demetra's abdomen. Right after this, Janice removed a brown tiger eye ring from Demetra's finger and took a leather hair barrette from a nearby table. Grasping these stolen trophies, Janice picked up Alexis and left the room to return to her room and wash away the blood. Danny merely stepped over to the sink in the room and began to wash the blood from his hands. In the process, he glanced over and saw a yellow cylindrical object lying on the vanity. He picked up the object and in one final act of humiliation, he thrust it into Demetra's vagina and exited the room.

The couple now had to decide what to do next. One thing was for sure, they couldn't stay at the motel. They did not own a car, but they knew they needed a quick exit. They decided to take Demetra's car and flee south. First, they had to get rid of any evidence. Danny would later claim that they took their blood-soaked clothes and threw them in the dumpsters behind the truck stop. As they drove south on Interstate 75, Janice rolled down the window and threw the knife out somewhere between Carbondale and the next exit south. None of these items would ever be found.

Chapter 7

When one stepped into Room 253, he or she would see the typical motel room. To the left of the doorway was a table with two chairs. On the right running along the wall was a waist-high cabinet with a flat top. This served as both a shelf and four drawers for storage. In the far left corner was the double bed with a small nightstand to the left which housed the rotary phone and one small drawer which contained a Gideon Bible.

The walls of the room directly in front of you were covered in a sage-colored wallpaper with a cluster of bamboo reeds providing an accent on the wall leading into the bathroom area. There was a vanity that took up the wall space directly across from the entrance. To the left, there was a small enclosed area containing a tub and a commode. Demetra had tried to make her small space homier but all that remained now was the last remnants of her moving out.

Chambracant Patel owned and operated the Country Boy Inn. It had been in his possession for the past eighteen months. On the morning of September 3, Mr. Patel found himself glancing up at the clock and noticing the time. It was around 10:00 a.m., and he had yet to see his tenant, Demetra Parker. He knew that Demetra was scheduled to check out that morning, but he had seen no signs of her.

Just a few minutes prior to this, Mr. Patel had found the keys belonging to Room 243 lying on his desk. He was unaware of how they got there. Usually, when he finds a key like this in the office, it indicates to him that the occupants of the room have checked out. He thought to himself that this was very unusual since the couple occupying that room were not scheduled to check out until September 8th. Mr. Patel asked his wife Manju, his children Cheta, Bhumika, and Chirag, as well as the housekeeper, Clint McDonald, how the keys got there and no one seemed to know. Janice would later say she had no idea how those keys ended up there either. She claimed that as she and Danny were making their escape, they realized the office was closed and for a brief moment panicked because they didn't know what to do with the key. She and Danny exchanged glances, and she jerked the keys from his grasp and flung them across the parking lot.

Mr. Patel ascended the steps on the back side of the hotel and made his way to Room 253. Mr. Patel thought that Demetra might need help with the last bit of her luggage and decided to check on her. An article in "Inside Detective" magazine described what the owner found.

> "Mr. Patel was shocked by what he saw. The room was in total shambles. Chairs lay on their sides. There were towels on the floor. The bureau drawers were open. A TV set had been knocked over. The bed was messy. There were dark red spots on it that looked suspicious – like blood.
>
> The manager moved deeper into the room, aghast at its condition. This was not Demetra Parker's doing. She was not an untidy girl.
>
> On the floor on the other side of the bed the man found the answer. His eyes widened in horror. His jaws went slack as he stared down at the nude body of 19-year-old Demetra Parker.
>
> Her arms were still in a lightweight robe. She lay

face up. Her body was almost completely covered with blood. The man backed away from the grisly sight. He left the room running and called the Whitfield County Sheriff's Office, gasping the grim details into the phone."

Walker Young and Dean Lemke of Dalton Ambulance Company were the first ones to arrive on the scene. Mr. Patel allowed Mr. Young to enter the room. When Walker Young entered the motel room, he found the bed pulled away from the wall at a forty-five degree angle, and he encountered the lifeless body of Demetra Parker. He then exited the room and told Mr. Patel that he needed to call a deputy. The ambulance drivers also contacted Leon Helton, the coroner for Whitfield County, to pronounce the body dead. When Helton arrived, he found Detective Don Gribble, Detective David Gordon, GBI Agent Bill Dodd and GBI Agent Charlie Johnson. He arrived on the scene at 11:30 a.m. and was there till 2 p.m.

Mr. Helton described Demetra as lying in a large pool of blood, but there was no blood on the furniture. However, there was some blood splatter on the walls. Hair was clutched in the victim's hands. Her legs were open and rigor mortis had set in. Mr. Helton couldn't say if any of the wounds had been inflicted while Miss Parker was upright.

Trying to decide who had caused the vicious death of Demetra Parker, the authorities quickly congregated both inside and out the motel. GBI agent Charles Johnson happened to be at the Sheriff's Department talking with Detective David Gordon when the call came into the department. Detective Gordon asked Agent Johnson to accompany him to the scene of the crime.

Johnson stated that when the pair arrived on the scene, they began collecting evidence. He took the sheets from the bed and the towels from the scene and placed them together in an evidence bag. He then turned to the overflowing ashtray that was on the table in the room. He picked out five Marlboro cigarette butts and placed them in an evidence bag. When he was later asked about removing just five butts from the ashtray, he replied that he only took the Marlboro ones because Demetra's boyfriend stated she did not smoke that particular brand. The agents also collected a bloody pair of panties lying next to the victim. Fingerprints were lifted from Coke cans, the vanity, the table, and any surface they thought they could obtain a print from. Detective Gribble took photos of the crime scene with both a 35 mm camera and a SX-70 Polaroid camera. The film was taken to Finley Studio for developing and the photos were sent to the district attorney's office.

Soon after being notified, Henry Wallace, the boyfriend of Demetra Parker, had arrived on the scene. Although, overcome with grief, Henry was cooperative with authorities and willing to do anything he could do help then find the killer or killers. He pointed out to the officers that Demetra's 1975 Buick Riviera was missing from the motel parking lot. Mr. Patel was asked about the car and if any other tenants had recently checked out of the motel. He stated that he had found the key to Room 243 in his office that morning and that the young couple occupying that room was paid up through the end of the week. He did say that he had seen the two the day before with Demetra. However, he stated that he had seen no signs of that couple or their young child that morning.

Also interviewed was George Dunnigan, whose room backed up to Demetra's room. He acknowledged he had heard noises coming from Demetra's room and the sound of a baby crying. This was sometime around 4:00 a.m. but Mr. Dunnigan stated that he did not contact anyone.

Moody Connell was the editor of the Dalton Daily Citizen and just happened to be in the sheriff's office when the call came through. In the book, "*Ladies Who Kill*," the author described Moody Connell's view of the scene. "Moody Connell kept hoping someone would cover the girl up with a blanket, a bed sheet, anything that might offer her some small, final dignity".

Mr. Patel went to the motel office, retrieved the key to the Buttrum's room, and allowed the deputies to enter. One of the first things they saw was a towel with what looked like blood spots lying near the bathroom sink. On the nearby desk, authorities found a birth certificate issued to Alexis with apparent blood stains on it as well. A quick glance around the room indicated that the tenants had left quite hastily. Could they have been the ones to commit this horrific crime and taken off in the victim's car? Fingerprints were taken off the table, beer cans, and Coke cans that were in the room. The agents also picked up four Marlboro cigarette packs.

Agent Johnson and Detective Gordon began questioning nearby friends and neighbors. It wasn't long before they found themselves at the Phillip 66 Truck Stop talking to James Teems. James had known Danny Buttrum prior to his working at the Phillip 66. Danny had worked for him previously in Adairsville, and James was familiar with his family there. He told the authorities that Danny's mother Evelyn still resided in Adairsville, and she should be able to tell them how to find Danny.

Willard Dodd was called in to assist Agent Johnson. He soon found himself standing on the doorsteps of Evelyn Buttrum's residence. She stated that Janice Buttrum had contacted her on September 2nd asking her for help with rent money. The couple needed $20 to help pay for their lodging at the Country Boy Inn. At first, Evelyn was not very forthcoming about information on the whereabouts of the young couple. As always, she was trying to protect her baby boy, Danny. Evelyn told authorities that Danny would never do anything like this unless Janice had talked him into it. Finally, after being threatened with obstruction of justice, Evelyn began to come clean about what she knew. She had seen the couple in the early morning hours of the September 3. They were in a car she had not seen before and only Janice had gotten out of the car to get money. Evelyn stated that the couple was headed south to Florida and would more than likely be calling her soon for more funds.

Part IV

“You have the right to remain silent.”

Chapter 8

Danny and Janice found themselves headed south to Pensacola, Florida. Hopefully there, they could escape the long arm of the law. Once they arrived in Pensacola, the couple again contacted Evelyn for more money. Danny had Janice call his mom and ask her to send $25 to the local Western Union office. Evelyn was beginning to crack under the pressure. She deeply felt her son was involved in something very bad. Did she continue to help him as she had always done, or did she turn him over to authorities? The choice weighed heavily on her heart, but finally, she reached out again to Agent Johnson and let him know the whereabouts of Danny and Janice.

It was at this point that Agent Frederick J. McFaul of the FBI became involved. On the morning of September 4, McFaul was contacted by the Jacksonville office and told that a Federal Unlawful Flight to Avoid Prosecution Warrant had been issued for both Danny and Janice. He was given a physical description of the couple, as well as the vehicle they could possibly be driving. He and Agent Howard Cargill were sent in the direction of Pensacola.

Meanwhile, Danny and Janice were acting like caged animals. Both were pacing back and forth waiting to hear from Evelyn. There were no cell phones or pagers to transmit information, so the couple sat parked beside a pay phone waiting to hear if Evelyn would once again bail them out. The call finally came, and Evelyn assured them that the money would be arriving shortly.

The couple hurriedly made their way to Romano Street to the local Western Union office. Danny told Janice to go into the nearby Newberry Department Store and pick up a couple of hamburgers. He would stay in the car and keep an eye on Alexis. Shortly after Janice entered the store, two local Pensacola police officers approached Danny and arrested him.

Janice described the scene as if it were playing out on a giant movie screen. She went inside the Newberry Department Store and placed an order for burgers at the fountain restaurant for Danny and her. She was waiting near the register as the food was being prepared. Janice said that she immediately noticed two men in dark suits approaching her. With their suits and ties, they reminded her of Joe Friday and his sidekick from Dragnet. She could almost hear the words, “Just the facts, ma'am” as the pair approached. Instead, one of them identified himself as Agent McFaul and asked, “Are you Janice Buttrum?” It was then that her world begin to collapse around her as he placed handcuffs on her wrist and led her from the store.

After exiting the department store, Janice was placed in the custody of Agent Sammon and Officer Knowles and was transported to the local FBI office. When she was taken into custody, she returned the ring and hair clasp belonging to Demetra. However, there was no sign of remorse from Janice.

At this point, Demetra's car was impounded. The following items were seized from the car: one t-shirt with a “Kraft” emblem; one pair of women's blue jeans; three white washcloths; one pair of men's work trousers; one pair of men's light-blue slacks; and a checkbook and social security card belonging to Demetra Parker. The car was not dusted for fingerprints and was later picked up in Florida by Demetra's brother Kenny. The three washcloths had what appeared to be blood stains on them and were sent to the crime lab. The alleged murder weapon was not recovered. The rest of the contents along with the car were released to Kenny.

According to the FBI report, the suspects each had their own story to tell the authorities. Janice stated that she approached Demetra's door first and then Danny shoved his way in. The room was dark, so Janice closed the door and turned on the light. She confessed to the agents that she was the first one to stab Demetra, after taking the knife from Danny. Janice went on to describe that Demetra fell on the bed and Danny continued to wrestle with her. Her claim was that Demetra was still breathing when the couple exited the room.

Continuing with her account of the facts, Janice claimed that Danny originally had the knife in his possession. He was holding the knife to Demetra's head when Demetra was able to twist his hand. That is when Janice grabbed the knife from Danny's hand and began to stab Demetra.

Janice began to describe her husband's behavior to the authorities. She stated he had been using "black beauties" and "yellow jackets" and that he was something of a drug addict. Janice began to try to take all the blame at this point by telling the officers she was unsure if Danny even stabbed Demetra at all. She also claimed that the couple left the room at the same time, although Danny's version was that Janice left the room before he did. Janice explained that the couple was in the room for approximately an hour and said, "That girl didn't want to die."

Janice did admit to taking personal belongings from Demetra, including her ring and a hair clasp. She also took a washcloth from the room that she used to wipe Demetra's blood from her hands. She stumbled in her statement when she claimed Danny had also washed blood off his hands after stabbing Demetra. She stated that their original purpose of going to Demetra's room was only to scare her. She also explained to the agents that while she was stabbing Demetra that Danny was pleasuring himself. She finally stopped stabbing Demetra when she saw Demetra's eyes roll back in her head.

Danny's version of events were somewhat different from Janice's. He claimed that they went to Demetra's room in order for Janice to get a cigarette from Demetra. They both approached Miss Parker's room and when she opened the door, Danny took this opportunity to push his way into the room. He related that Janice closed the door and may have turned on the lights. He admitted to struggling with Demetra and that he was holding her down on the floor when Janice removed a knife from his right front pocket. She stabbed Demetra several times in the heart region through the top she was wearing. Danny then took the knife from Janice and stabbed Demetra. He claimed she screamed out briefly at this point. He also admitted to raping Demetra but that he was unable to complete the act.

Janice and Danny were incarcerated in Pensacola until officials could arrive from Dalton to transport them back. She remembered spending time in the cell and the jailer bringing religious material to her and thrusting it in through the bars. It was a series of books by Chaplain Ray, and he kept repeating to her that she needed to read them. Janice stated that at this point the magnitude of what she had done began to resonate inside her mind. She had taken a human life, and now she must face the consequences of her actions.

The authorities from Dalton, Sheriff Jack Davis and

Detective David Gordon, arrived to take Danny and Janice back to Dalton, Georgia. The two were transported together in the back of a squad car. Danny, a seasoned veteran of being in the back of a patrol car, chose to keep his mouth closed. Janice, on the other hand, was being a typical teenage girl or else working out nervous energy by talking almost constantly without taking a breath. At one point, Janice leaned up to get Sheriff Davis's attention and asked him. "Aren't you suppose to feel remorse when you kill someone?" As she said this, she looked over at Danny, hoping to do something to get a response. After getting no reaction, she huffed and leaned back, stating, "I don't feel anything." Who knows if that is truly how she felt or if it was her rebellious teenage spirit.

Once the pair arrived in Dalton, they came under the watchful eye of the Georgia Bureau of Investigation. Again, their attitudes were much different in how they interacted with law enforcement. There were three men present, GBI Agent Charles Johnson, Detective David Gordon, and Sheriff Jack Davis while each were questioned. Agent Johnson was primarily the one in charge of the questioning.

The agents began with questioning the one they thought would talk the most. Janice's interview started with the usual Miranda rights. Janice assured the agents that she already knew them by heart and recited the familiar phrase verbatim to the FBI agents. She boastfully bragged that she had learned them from watching TV. Janice was eager to answer the agent's questions and he began by asking her how long she had been at the Country Boy Inn. She stated they had been living there approximately two weeks. When asked, she eagerly related the events from earlier in the day when she and Demetra had spent time at the laundry mat together until they returned to the hotel together.

Agent Johnson asked for the purpose of going to Demetra's room. She replied that she and Danny just wanted to scare her. Just prior to this, they had been sitting in their room talking about their mothers. In the recorded interview, Janice stated, "Danny was going to act like he was going to cut her, when he went into the room and grabbed her." She claimed that the entire plan was a practical joke that had gone terribly wrong. Janice tried to protect Danny when she said Demetra had gotten the knife away from her husband Danny and had tried to stab him. That was when Janice grabbed the knife from Demetra's hand and began stabbing her. When asked how many times that she had stabbed Demetra, she couldn't give an actual number. Janice stated she just kept stabbing her over and over because she just wouldn't die.

When Agent Johnson asked Janice if it was wrong to kill someone, she stated that she knew the Bible said it was wrong but to her it wasn't. Agent Johnson asked her why and she replied, "Because it's not wrong for someone to rape a prisoner, it's not wrong for you to kill an animal so why should it be wrong to kill a person." Yet, in the next statement, she said she felt it was wrong to rape somebody.

She continued to state her opinion about murder, "People kill other people all the time." Agent Johnson asked her if that made it right. She replied, "No. If it's not wrong for the judge to say we are going to put this man in the electric chair, no, it's not wrong for anybody to kill somebody else." Again, Janice denied having any kind of sexual relations with Demetra but did admit to making the cut that caused the gaping wound on her abdomen. Ownership of this final gruesome act would change periodically to suit whoever was telling the story. The conversation with Janice lasted approximately forty-five minutes.

The agents then moved to Danny. The first question they asked him was "Do you want to talk to us?" He was quick to answer, "She did, didn't she." He also persisted with the excuse that the only reason they went to Demetra's room was to scare her. Danny confirmed that Janice had approached Demetra's door and asked for a cigarette, and when she answered the door, Danny forced his way into the room.

Danny began to explain how he grabbed Demetra but that she had gotten a knife and tried to stab him with it. He then described how Janice had his knife and had stabbed Demetra. Danny claimed that he shoved Demetra to the floor, but he was not the one who initiated the knife attack. However, neither he nor the detectives could account for the knife that Demetra supposedly had. This additional knife was also never found. Danny was quick to place all blame on his wife as he told the agent that Janice had delivered the first stab wound. He did admit to also stabbing Demetra but could not remember how many times that this had occurred.

Next, Danny tried to imply that he was crazy. When asked about this, he replied, "I just am, I ain't got no sense about nothing. I mean you don't have to take my word you can ask my mother or ask anybody." Again, he apparently thought maybe his mom would come to his rescue. Danny was also asked how he felt about killing Demetra. His reacted by stating, "I don't feel bad about it, if that's what you are talking about." Danny concluded the interrogation by once again placing the blame on Janice for the final gash across Demetra's abdomen. He also claimed not to know the location of the murder weapon; he would only say that it had been thrown out in the median somewhere between Dalton and Atlanta.

Danny was later asked if he thought that Janice was bisexual. This question had come up earlier in Janice's interview and she had denied this. Once again, Danny denied having had sexual intercourse with Demetra. He stated that he would willingly take a lie detector test to prove this. His interview, lasting a mere fifteen minutes, was brief compared to Janice's.

The following is the statements made by Janice to the FBI regarding the events surrounding the death of Demetra Parker.

"I, Janice Marie Buttrum, furnish the following information in the form of a signed statement to James W. Sammon and Frederick J. McFaul, who I know to be Special Agents of the FBI. I furnish this information freely and voluntarily. I have been promised nothing.

I am a white female, age 17, having been born January 17, 1964 at Calhoun, Ga. I reside at Route 3, Adairsville, GA with my husband Danny Buttrum.

Sometime after midnight, Wednesday, September 3, 1980, I went to Room 253 at the Country Boy Inn, Carbondale Road, Dalton, Ga. This was the room of 'Dedra' or 'Dee' Parker. I was staying in Room 243 at that motel.

The purpose of my visit was to scare her, however she began screaming. I took a pocket knife and began stabbing her in an effort to kill her. I cannot state just how many times I stabbed her, but I was in the room about one hour.

I took a ring from Dee's finger and her purse from the room.

Danny Buttrum accompanied me in this act. When Danny entered Dee's room, he grabbed her and she screamed. Danny had the knife in his hand and Dee tested his hand. This is when I took the knife and began stabbing Dee. At one point, Danny also stabbed Dee.

The Buick Electra that I used to drive to Pensacola was Dee's and was stolen after we killed her.

I have read this statement consisting of this and on other page and it is true and correct to the best of my knowledge."

Danny's statement was similar in that he placed the weapon in Janice's hand first. However, there was something that the pair had disagreed on. Danny claimed to the agents that Janice had expressed an interest in wanting to be with Demetra in a sexual way. Janice was quick to dispel this rumor.

While conducting interviews for this book, the author spoke with one of the law enforcement officers involved, and the first thing he said was, "Did you know Janice was bisexual?" He said this as if he was sharing a tantalizing bit of gossip. Further research would reveal the source of this gossip. When Janice was having her sixty day mental evaluation, a psychologist asked Janice about whether she had homosexual ideations. Janice said that she did not and the expert brought up the fact that she had previously mentioned that she was bisexual. Janice stated that when she was in YDC, there had been another patient who was a lesbian and liked to taunt the other female patients. Another patient had mentioned to Janice that if the two acted as if they were couple that this particular patient would leave them alone. The plan created by the pair worked and they were not harassed. This ruse would cause Janice to gain the label of liking both men and women. Danny, however, later admitted to GBI agents that he did not think his wife was bisexual.

The following is Danny Buttrum's confession to the crime. WARNING: Graphic language

I, Danny Buttrum, make this free and voluntary statement to Fredrick J. McFaul and Howard W. Cowgill, who have identified themselves to me as Special Agents of the Federal

Bureau of Investigation. I am 28 years old having been born on September 25th, 1951 at Bartow County, Georgia. I have completed 8 years of education and I read and write the English language.

On September 2, 1980 which is a Tuesday. I was at the Country Boy Inn motel in Dalton, Georgia and I was with another person and we went to the room of a girl named Parker. She was in a room at the same motel we were staying. The woman with me knocked on Parker's door and asked for a cigarette. I pushed the door open and pushed Parker on the floor. The person I was with put the baby down on the floor, took a pocket knife out of my right front pants pocket and this person stabbed Parker 3 or 4 times. I got the knife and stabbed Parker several times. Parker was wearing slacks and a blouse. The person with me said "I want to eat her c***" or words to that effect. This person had already taken Parker's pants and panties off. This person then performed oral sex on Parker after that I had sexual intercourse with Parker but did not climax. After "screwing" Parker I went to the bathroom and washed my hands which had blood on them. When I returned into the room I saw the person stabbing Parker several times. This person then gave me the knife and I stabbed Parker several more times. I then stuck a hard plastic white object into Parker's vagina and me and the other person along with a baby left the room, stole Parker's car and drove to Pensacola, Florida. I have read this statement of this paper and one other paper and it is true and correct."

Chapter 9

Danny and Janice soon found themselves in separate jail cells under the watchful eye of Sheriff Jack Davis. The pair was given court appointed attorneys. Danny's attorneys were Greg Melton and Greg Brown. Janice was represented by Steve Fain. Janice described her first encounter with Mr. Fain. "He came to see me at the county jail and he was dressed in tennis clothes. It was Saturday and he introduced himself to me. He told me that he was really struggling about representing me. Steve said that some of the members of the church he was a member of were upset with him representing a murderer. He was struggling with doing the job that he loved and his moral conscience. He just kept saying he didn't know if he could do the job. His trepidation lasted until the day of the preliminary hearing. He asked Judge Pannell for a brief moment to collect his thoughts before committing to the task at hand. He walked out of the room and into the nearby law library. Returning in a few minutes, he told Judge Pannell he would accept the assignment. Janice asked him what had happened, and he simply said, 'I prayed'." After a preliminary hearing, the two were bound over to the grand jury. The grand jury charged Janice with Count 1 – murder and Count 2 -theft by taking in regard to taking Demetra's car.

Janice had a lot of time on her hands behind bars in the county jail. She was separated from her husband and her daughter, and she was soon faced with the realization that she was pregnant again. Janice picked up a pen and put some of her thoughts on paper. The following are three letters that were in intercepted by the authorities and definitely show that she was very much in love with Danny.

"Hi Baby,

How are you? Fine I hope. I'm okay but I sure do miss you. I really enjoyed seeing you Thursday. I'm going to tell my lawyer in no uncertain terms that I'm going on trial with you because we were together all the time and we've been together so far and I want to be with you for as long as I possibly can. Honey I love you so very, very, very, very, very much. I hope you get this letter because I want you to know how much I really love you because it would be easier for me to go to trial by myself but I don't want to. Danny please don't ever stop loving me because I need you so very much and I always will. We will be together outside one of these days I just know that we will. Honey this baby will be born sometime in July if I'm counting my month's right. Darling I'm going to make this letter short so you'll get it real soon. Baby I'll let you go till later. Write me back soon. Love ya always and forever.

Jan

Here's my heart, soul, love & kisses. Forever & ever & always."

The letter had a hand-drawn heart filled with x's.
The second letter was dated 9-25-80

"Hi Baby,

How are you? Fine I hope. I am doing okay but I sure do miss being with you. I went to court today for the judge to give me a copy of the unified appeal proceedings they were going to take you too but your attorney was in court with another case. I won't get to mail this till Saturday and you'll get it Monday or Tuesday but I got to thinking about you and decided to write it now. Felicia has gone to Hardwick and as of now I'm the only woman in jail. We go to our preliminaries next Thursday or at least I think we go together but I'm not sure if we do or not. I'll let you know when I see you if you're going to be Daddy again or not. I sure hope you are because this may be this last chance I have to have a son by you.

If you need any cigarettes tell the jailer and I'll send you some. I am going to buy another carton Saturday if your mama gives me 3 dollars. She sent me five yesterday and I spent just about one on cokes because I don't like that coffee or the other junk they give you to drink either. I hope you're eating this food because it certainly is better than what Bartow County feeds you. I hope you can read this because I'm trying to smoke a cigarette and write too and it's kinda hard to do. The reason I sent you a pack of cigarettes back the other day is "They had opened them and took whatever was in them out. So we might as well quit sending notes in cigarettes and just write each other. By the time you get this you'll have your stamps so you better write me back. My lawyer is going to try and get me manslaughter so I won't have to die young. Which means if he can do that I'll get 20 years and be up for parole in 7 but I don't think he can because the DA spoke at me like I was a very sick person today. I hope you're telling your lawyer the truth because it could help you. I also hope you feel sorry for what we've done because I do and if you don't there is something very much wrong with you. I'm not trying to be mean or sarcastic but that is the simple truth of the matter. Baby I still love you not as much as I did but I still love you and care about you so please be as good as possible and always remember me no matter what happens. I'm so afraid that this trial and everything is going to pull us so far apart that we'll never be able to get back together if we live through the next 20 years. Well I'll let you go for now and write later.

Love always,

Jan"

This letter again ends with a hand-drawn heart filled with x's.

Below the heart it read, "Here's my heart, soul, love and kisses forever."

What transpired in Janice's world in the next month or so is not certain, but obviously being separated from Danny and baby Alexis was beginning to take its toll on her. There were several theories of what could have transpired by this time. Evelyn Buttrum was continuing to bring baby Alexis to visit Janice in prison. She was sharing with Janice that Danny was running out of second chances. He was on the brink of serving some major time, but, Janice could save him. Because she was a minor, and a first time offender, she was looking at less time because of her age. She would still have a long life ahead of her. Evelyn swore to Janice that she would take good care of Alexis and the baby Janice was carrying. This visit began to weigh heavily on Janice's heart.

The next and final letter, dated November 3, held a much different tone. All of a sudden, Janice was willing to take all the blame. This letter was written to one of the jailers in hopes that it would go up the chain of command. The first few lines of the letter is illegible due to being copied numerous times but line three begins the essence of her plea.

> "I thought Danny was having sex with her but he wasn't. She (Demetra) was prettier than I was and I was afraid that she was going to take Danny away from me. I made Danny do everything that he done including raping her and I made him steal her car. My husband is guiltless of any wrong doing because he was coerced into doing everything that he done. I wasn't going to tell anyone this but I love Danny too much to let him die for what I made him do. So the motive for murder was and is unwanted jealousy.
>
> November 5, 1980
> Janice Marie Buttrum

I will take a polygraph to prove I'm not lying. Call Sheriff Davis if you think you should or call one of my lawyers or one of Danny's lawyers and get them down here together please."

Chapter 10

Near the end of September, Danny came under the radar of Hugh Don Smith. Hugh Don was a former used car salesman who had been convicted by the federal government. He had owned a used car lot in Rome, GA called Smith Auto Brokers. In 1979, Hugh Don was arrested and charged with 120 counts of receiving, transporting, and selling stolen motor vehicles. The first jury was a hung jury but a second jury had found him guilty of eighty counts. He asked that his incarceration be postponed for three months so he could get his affairs in order. In that three months, he basically went and pursued a nonstop spending spree. He bought expensive furniture for his home, a carrier to haul his cars to market, and also went on several gambling vacations. He cashed checks totaling $81,740 at the National City Bank in Rome, GA. Hugh Don was now serving his federal time within the confines of the Whitfield County Jail. It was there, that he volunteered his services to gain information from Danny Buttrum.

Chief Deputy Ray Swanson shared what life was like for Hugh Don behind bars. Because of Hugh Don's mechanical experience, he was made a trustee and was allowed to work on the sheriff's vehicle, as well as other officers' cars. It was not unusual to see Hugh Don out and about on a scooter picking up needed car parts. The attorneys for the defendants once stated they saw Hugh Don in the lobby of the jail talking on the pay phone, and there was no officer in sight. Probably the most humorous incident noted was that on visitation day

Hugh Don's wife and girlfriend both visited him at the same time. He would spend the time going to each one's window to visit over the phone without the other knowing.

Hugh Don volunteered his "services" to see if he could obtain any information from Danny Buttrum. He stated that Danny had approached him prior to September 25 when he saw Smith working on his own case. Danny asked Hugh Don if he knew anything about the law to which Hugh Don replied, "A little." Danny then suggested, "I want you to see if I qualify to be crazy."

Danny was on suicide watch because he had attempted to scratch his wrists with a broken BIC pen, and Hugh Don suggested that Danny could hang out in his cell during the day. He could keep a watch on Danny and see if could get Danny to share his secrets all at the same time. According to officials, Hugh Don was offered no deals for his participation.

Danny was quick to brag about what he thought he could get by with concerning his attack on Demetra. One of the first things he stated was that he thought officials would be unable to prove that he had raped Demetra based on the fact they would be unable to find sperm in the vagina. Autopsy reports would confirm this claim. Danny based this information on two things: 1) he was unable to conclude the act because his wife was watching him and 2) he had been taking speed. Danny also related to Hugh Don that he acted out of jealousy when he went to Demetra's room to attack her. However, Danny would later testify that he could not recall sharing this information with Mr. Smith. Also questioned at the same time, Hugh Don would admit that he had been caught lying on the stand on previous occasions.

Chapter 11

Judge Charles Pannell, Jr. was chosen to preside over the proceedings regarding Danny and Janice Buttrum. He had only been a Superior Court Judge about eighteen months. District Attorney Steve Williams was seeking the death penalty for the pair. Later, Judge Pannell would admit that he had presided over three death penalty cases in his entire career as both a local and a federal judge. The first two were the Buttrums and later Eric Rudolph, the man convicted of the bombing of Olympic Park in Atlanta and various abortion clinics across the South.

One of the first things that Judge Pannell did was to request a 60-day mental evaluation for both defendants. Their examinations were to be done at Central State Hospital in Milledgeville. The exams would determine if the two were mentally capable to stand trial for the crime they had committed.

In Janice's examination, a vivid description of her wretched childhood began to unfold. Janice was born to Marie Beavers who "sold" her to R.V. and Elizabeth Adcock in exchange for the couple paying the mother's outstanding hospital bill. Her biological father was unknown. Prior to Janice living with the Adcocks, Elizabeth had a son who died prematurely. For a long time after his death, she washed and ironed the baby clothing as if the child were still living. Mrs. Adcock would tell people that she had bought Janice and that Janice belonged to her.

Both of the Adcocks had heavy drinking problems.

According to a Bartow DEFACS worker, there were times that Mrs. Adcock appeared emotionally unstable. There were also incidents of suspected neglect and abuse of Janice. Mrs. Rose, who was a Public Health Nurse, saw Elizabeth verbally abuse Janice on multiple occasions.

Neglect became obviously noticeable when Janice entered school. Teachers described her as unkempt and dirty. She was dressed in clothes that her family had gotten from the city dump. Because of this students made fun of her and noticeably avoided her because of her terrible body odor.

Janice married Danny Buttrum when she was fifteen years old. Twice between December 1978 and May 1979, relatives took out warrants against Danny for physically abusing Janice. Janice claimed that Danny had violent headaches and "went wild". He did not remember abusing her after these beatings. Mike Fowler, Danny's probation officer backed up this information stating that Danny drank excessively and that his violent behavior broke up his first marriage to a woman named Candy. Janice stated that she felt that the only three people who really loved her were her father, Danny, and her baby.

Mr. Adcock died in the summer of 1976. This was the parent with whom Janice seemed to have a closer personal relationship. Shortly thereafter, Mrs. Adcock moved another man into the residence. It was at this point that Janice began to run away from home.

Beginning in October, 1976, Janice was placed in several foster homes, one group home, and also the home of a neighbor. She was unable to settle herself into any of these different settings. Janice refused to go to school, had temper tantrums, would not accept discipline, was destructive and had a history of running away. She was returned to her mother for a short period of time. Mrs. Adcock was living in a small travel trailer with her boyfriend. There were allegations involving physical abuse with Mrs. Adcock and sexual abuse involving the boyfriend.

In March, 1977, Janice moved in with a neighbor, but this arrangement did not last long. She would sneak out of this home without permission and was accused of stealing items from the neighbor. On March 23, Janice ran away with two males and admitted to having sexual intercourse with both males. (This information is verified in an early chapter when Janice wrote about wanting to run away to Atlanta and become a prostitute.) Due to her actions, she was placed in the Rome detention center and later transferred to the Macon Youth Development Center on May 11, 1977.

Janice stayed in Macon for six months. A release summary stated that Janice had improved in her relationships with her peers and also her self-image. When she left Macon YDC, she entered the Georgia Industrial Home in Macon. This was a private institution, and they reluctantly accepted her as a non-paying resident. Mr. Ashley Cox, the administrator of this home, described Janice as getting along with the staff and one who did her assigned duties well. She had attended eighth grade classes at Lanier A High School, where she had fair grades. Nevertheless, she dropped out of school not long after this.

Janice was again asked about her sexual orientation. She denied ever having any homosexual relationships although previous reports mentioned that Janice might be bisexual. Janice again explained this to the examiner. She restated that when she was at YDC, there was a girl who was afraid of the homosexual girls. The girl stated that if these girls thought she was going with someone else they would leave her alone. Janice said for this reason, she agreed to say that she and this girl were going together. Janice later told Danny of this incidence and that he shared this with his mother Evelyn. She believed the entire episode was just taken the wrong way.

It was also determined from previous records that Mrs. Elizabeth Adcock had a brother who had been at Central State Hospital. After speaking with two family members, relatives of the Adcocks, they both stated that Janice was "kept" by her parents but was not born into the family. Mr. Odell Adcock, a cousin to Ralph Adcock, described Janice as a loner and he stated that he felt Danny was not good to her.

In the Impressions/Recommendations section of the report from Central State, it was revealed that informants felt that Janice was capable of committing a violent crime, but they also had compassion for her. Most of them stated "she never had a chance." They felt she was a victim of a deplorable home environment and that she had developed the anti-social traits as a coping mechanism. All of the people who were interviewed seemed to think that Janice ultimately lacked a conscience and had no fear of consequences. She was unable to form close relationships with others. All of them felt that her relationship with Danny had only added to the problem.

The only tears that Janice shed were when she told the examiners that she was "scared to death." Her biggest fear was losing Danny. Also, she didn't want to spend the rest of her life waiting to be executed and she certainly didn't want her children growing up without a mother the way she did. Examiners found her competent to return to court and face the charges against her.

Chapter 12

Danny was the next one occupy the seat across from the examiner. On the evaluation form under the category 'present mental illness', Danny complained of chronic headaches over the past six to seven years. He stated that things had happened to him as a child, and he had let those feelings build up inside. He alluded to the fact that when these feelings built up he had a tendency to act out on them, but he did not say how.

When asked about the murder of Demetra Parker, Danny said he had been working at the truck stop at Carbondale for two weeks. He stated that his employer wanted the weekend off, so he had volunteered to work from Friday night until Monday morning. When he got off work at 9:00 a.m. on Monday morning; Danny remembered taking a shower and sending Janice to purchase beer for him. He washed down six black beauties with the beer. Danny claimed that he could remember nothing from 3:00 p.m. on Monday to 10:00 a.m. on Wednesday after the murder. The next thing he was able to remember was being in Pensacola. He asked Janice how he got there. She reminded him that he had driven there, but he did not question whose car they were driving. Shortly thereafter, they were arrested by the FBI.

Danny had previously been hospitalized for mental illness at Rome Regional Hospital for two weeks. Notes from that stay indicated some depression due to drug abuse. However, the present exam revealed no signs of psychosis.

When looking into Danny's mental history, the notes

indicated he was also admitted to Northwest Georgia Regional Hospital in July, 1977. At that time, Danny was having paranoid ideations, homicidal feelings toward his mother, and an obsession with sex. He had attempted to attack his mother with a butcher knife two weeks prior to this hospitalization, but he denied this ever occurred. During this hospitalization, he expressed to the examiners that he was having an unreasonable urge to randomly rape women. He also described the feeling of wanting to kill someone. The diagnosis at the time was depressive neurosis and ruling out Acute Schizophrenic Episode. Evelyn, his mother, was present for these interviews. It is also interesting to note that Danny was scheduled for a revocation of his probation hearing just after this voluntary hospitalization. The hospital assumed that the stress of his court appearance had triggered his ingestion of unprescribed medications which led to his being admitted.

At the time of the 1977 evaluation, Evelyn stated Danny had been having mental problems for four years. She described her son was suffering from spells that she characterized as him "losing his mind". During these past episodes, he had become very destructive and had broken furniture, windows and caused damage to the family car. Evelyn stated that Danny often did not remember anything that happened during these spells.

Evelyn denied the fact that her son used drugs. However she stated that he did take "speed" the day before Demetra's murder. She stated that he had only been drinking the past six years and that he had hand tremors when he was not drinking. Evelyn also revealed a family history of mental illness. Danny's father had been a patient at Central State Hospital in 1960 because of "severe headaches" and "mental retardation." Evelyn felt strongly that Danny would not have committed murder had he been in his right mind.

Further questioning of Danny revealed that he usually drank a half case of beer on the weekends, but he denied drinking during the week. He had been drinking since he was sixteen years old. Prior to his previous hospitalization, Danny was drinking two and half pints of liquor a month. He stated he had experienced hand tremors when he was consuming that much alcohol but was not conscious of having them since. Danny described a three-week history of using "speed" prior to the murder on September 3. He was taking approximately four pills a day but the day before murder, he admitted to taking six. Danny also admitted to having "spells" and that he is not aware of his actions during these episodes. He also stated that he had threatened and physically harmed his wife on several occasions and his mother on one occasion. In addition, he claimed to have experienced auditory hallucinations for the past six months. He revealed that these voices say, "I'm going to get you and destroy you." He also reported that he had attempted suicide on four separate occasions, the most recent one occurring while he was in the Whitfield County jail.

Danny described his childhood as good, although he felt his parents had a bad marriage. He stated that his mother frequently cursed at his father for "running around" with his first wife. He quit school at fifteen because he said his teachers told him he was slow. He also got into trouble at school for fighting. This need to address his problems physically may have played a major part in Danny's first marriage which ended in divorce. His current marriage seemed to have been following the same destructive path as the first.

Danny was aware of the current charges against him although he stated that he had no recollection of the crime. However, one of the nursing staff stated that Danny has shared his version of the events with another patient at the facility. He alleged that the last thing he remembered was going into Demetra's hotel room, and then after that he remembered traveling to Florida. Danny stated that Janice was the one who told him what to say to the police prior to their being arrested.

Intelligence tests performed on Danny indicated a verbal score of 72 and a performance score of 80. This demonstrated an IQ of approximately 74, a normal IQ is considered 80. He was also given the Minnesota Multiphasic Personality Inventory and it was indicative of "Faking bad." In other words, he was trying to present himself in the worse possible light. He was diagnosed with the following: 1) Antisocial personality, 2) Drug dependence, other psycho-stimulus (amphetamines), 3) Habitual Excessive Drinking, 4) Borderline Range of Intelligence, with possible organic impairment. There was no evidence of a learning disability. Ward personnel have also indicated that Mr. Buttrum was "playing crazy." There were no psychotic symptoms noted during his clinical interview.

The examiner felt that Danny was well aware of the charges against him and should be returned to Dalton to stand trial.

Part V
The State vs Janice and Danny Buttrum

Chapter 13

In February, 1981, the competency trial began for Janice Buttrum. Both she and Danny would have a competency trial to see if they were mentally competent to participate in a criminal trial. Judge Pannell presided over both competency trials and both criminal trials. Janice was in the second trimester of her pregnancy. She had been incarcerated since her arrest in September, 1980, except for the sixty-nine days she had spent at Central State Hospital.

As Judge Pannell was opening the trial, he noted that a group of high school students sponsored by the local Rotary Club had come to observe the proceedings. He took a few moments to explain the purpose of a competency trial and the role of the district attorney. Then he allowed Attorney Steve Fain to begin his opening statement. What must these high school students have been thinking to see this young lady, basically their own age, being on trial for such a horrific crime!

Mr. Fain arose from his chair and began his opening statement by explaining the difference between a competency trial and a criminal trial. The jurors would not be determining Janice's guilt or innocence, only whether or not she was competent to stand trial. This was followed by a brief history of Janice's tumultuous childhood beginning with her being "sold" to R.V. and Elizabeth Adcock. He also added that in 1976, the state alleged that Janice was a deprived child under the laws of Georgia. This was followed by several foster homes, group homes, a short stint with relatives and finally her marriage to

Danny Buttrum at the age of fifteen. Janice may have unfortunately viewed Danny as her knight in shining armor after all she had been through in her life up to this point.

The first person called to testify was Carol Rose, a registered nurse with the Northwest Georgia Regional Hospital. When she first became involved with Janice, she was a Public Health Nurse for Bartow County. Mrs. Rose had been a registered nurse since 1954. The first time Carol came in contact with Janice was 1968, soon after she began working for Bartow County. Janice was only five years old at the time. Mrs. Rose was originally set to see Elizabeth Adcock, who had both skin and visual problems. Carol saw Janice on a relatively consistent basis, and her overall opinion was that Janice was misplaced. She described the three room home that Janice was living in as well as Janice's unkempt condition.

Carol described how Mrs. Adcock was more than willing to share how they acquired Janice. Mr. Barton, the owner of the local funeral home, acted as a facilitator between the Adcocks and the hospital and helped them bring baby Janice home. A formal adoption agreement was never made, but Janice went home with the Adcocks after they paid the mother's hospital bill. Mrs. Rose maintained that the chronological age of the Adcocks and their alcoholic history did not make them ideal candidates for parenthood. She felt that Janice only became worse with time instead of better. Carol felt strongly that Mr. Adcock was the glue that held the family together, as he provided the basic necessities of life. However, after his death, the family unit quickly fell apart. After his death, Mrs. Adcock sold the family home, and she and Janice moved into an 8 x 30 travel trailer. The physical condition of the home environment declined considerably.

Carol gave a detailed picture of the relationship between

Elizabeth Adcock and Janice. She felt that Elizabeth was very overbearing with Janice. When Carol came to visit, Elizabeth would have a switch in her hand, and if she felt that Janice was sharing too much information, she would strike her with the switch. Elizabeth would also use foul language toward Janice that Carol did not feel was appropriate. She would also compare Janice to her mother and often state that she would grow up to be just like her. She even went as far as calling Janice's mother a whore.

Carol stated that she had a good relationship with Janice and that she had children who were the same age as Janice. When there were school vacations, Janice would even spend several days at Carol's house. Carol went on to describe Janice as being "severely deprived." She did not feel that Janice's basic emotional needs were met by the Adcocks. Carol's perception was that the Adcocks loved Janice but did not teach her basic social skills.

Mary Caruthers, Janice's fourth grade teacher at Adairsville Elementary School, followed Mrs. Rose to the witness stand. Mary described Janice as a loner but that she was not a discipline problem. She stated that the other students made fun of her because of her body odor and her unkempt appearance. Mary described Janice's hair as being matted and her clothes being filthy. The children would taunt her about seeing her at the city dump. Many children claimed to see her there with her family scavenging the garbage. Ms. Caruthers stated that Janice had slightly below average grades of C's and D's. She continued to describe Janice in the following way, "Her pants were too large for her; shirts that were men's shirts. She did not dress like an average child, wear dresses, you know, and have her hair clean. It was just a mat – her hair was always matted and you couldn't tell if she were – just what color she was, because her face was just so dirty."

Ms. Caruthers went on to say that Janice was never properly dressed for the weather conditions. She described Janice as being emotionally immature. She stated that Janice was bullied extensively by other students who were not in her classroom. They would surround her on the playground and taunt her about the way she looked and dressed. Janice was a passive child and took the bullying by her peers. Janice would just try to ignore them.

Mrs. Caruthers had only met the Adcocks on one occasion when they unexpectedly arrived to her home. She could not remember any reason for the meeting. However, she went on to state that she, too, felt that the Adcocks had not taught Janice basic social skills nor were they fulfilling her emotional needs. She described her as an average student. Mrs. Caruthers did state that she had not interacted with Janice since she left her classroom except for the occasional time when they would encounter each other in public, such as the grocery store or the gas station. Mary stated that in her entire seventeen years of teaching that Janice stands out as the most deprived child that she had ever had.

Janice's fifth grade teacher, Rose Johnson ascended to the stand next. She agreed with Mrs. Caruthers's statement about Janice being a loner and that she had not been a discipline problem. Rose reiterated that the other students made fun of her clothes and her personal appearance. She claimed that she had not had interactions with the Adcocks regarding Janice during the school year. Mrs. Johnson also described Janice as one of the worst deprived children she had seen in her twenty-seven years of teaching.

Mrs. Tommy West, who served as the librarian and later in the office at Adairsville Elementary School, described her interactions with Janice. She had known Janice since she entered the first grade in 1969 and continued until 1976. In her role as librarian, she saw Janice on an average of two to three times a week. When she moved to the office, she saw Janice on a daily basis as she observed her and other students in the hallways during class change. Mrs. West stated that she saw Janice as a loner, and her physical appearance was very unkempt. She also stated that it seemed Janice was unable to interact with the other children. Mrs. West stated that she'd had no personal interactions with Janice since 1976.

Mr. Marvin Dickerson, the social worker for Bartow County Schools, described how he first encountered Janice in 1976. Janice had been referred to him because of her ongoing truancy. Marvin had visited the Adcock home on several occasions and Elizabeth had again described how she had bought Janice and owned her. Their "home" was a travel trailer measuring 8 feet wide by 30 feet long, and he described it as being in total disarray. On his third visit to the home, he found Janice at the home. He noted that her physical appearance was very unkempt. Marvin asked her if she was living in the trailer, and she replied that she was staying in a broken down van which was adjacent to the trailer. Janice told him that whenever she got clean clothes, her mother took them away from her and put them in the corner for their dog to lie on. Janice stated she slept in the van just to take care of herself.

The court recessed at this point for lunch. When court reconvened at 1:15 p.m., Mr. Dickerson continued where he left off describing the deplorable conditions he had experienced when interacting with Janice and her mother.

Marvin was asked to describe the conditions there since he had experienced it firsthand. "I think the one word that best describes it is filthy, which was the condition I found Janice in.

I don't think you can say any more than filthy. I mean, it was - - it was really nasty. Mrs. Adcock obviously didn't take care of herself; Mr. Peace (the boyfriend) looked like he was a couple of weeks away from a bath; and Janice looked worse than that. I mean, she was expected to fend for herself out there. I asked Mrs. Adcock would it be okay for me to take Janice somewhere and get her some clothes - - and this was between 5:00 and 6:00 in the afternoon - - and she said, 'Yeah, if she wants to go with you, it'll be all right with me.' I took her on. I went to my superintendent's secretary's house - - she has some girls about Janice's size - - and we were over there a couple of hours while Mrs. Reed cut down some of her own daughter's clothes to fit Janice, and then my wife and I took her out to eat that night before we returned her home."

Marvin stated that he used the truancy charges as a way to get Janice out of the home and get her some help. He felt that Mrs. Adcock was negligent in her care of Janice. When he got Mrs. Adcock to court, she remarked to Janice, "I hate you and I never want to see you again." The judge ordered Janice removed from the home. Marvin said Janice was the most neglected child he had ever seen in his life.

Marvin further described Janice as a follower. He stated that she was not a leader in any way, shape, or form. He felt that Janice was a child who just needed to be loved. Marvin stated that the best way to describe her would be one who was totally rejected. At a previous custody hearing for Janice, Judge Bert Craine refused to see Janice until she had an attorney to represent her. In the meantime, she was taken in by the Haney's, a couple who lived across the street from the trailer park. She was only there a day or two before she ran away. When Marvin investigated the situation, he determined that she had spent the night with two 27-year-old men. Of course, Janice was only fourteen at that time and looking for the first person who would show her love and affection. Janice described this same situation in her journal and wrote that is when she was looking for some means to make her way in the world.

Mr. Dickerson also testified about Marie Beavers, Janice's biological mother. "The person who was her mother was named Beavers. Ms. Beavers had children by a number of different fathers, and whenever the children became of age - - were born, rather, she just gave them away to whoever would pay their doctor bill. Sometimes she just gave them away. I've dealt with three of those children. Mrs. Beavers had eight children in her lifetime."

During Marvin's testimony, he described one other situation that he encountered in the Adcock home. "One of the times I went over to the trailer, I noted that Mr. Peace had his fingernails all painted bright red, which I thought was sort of strange for a man forty-five years old, with a grizzly beard. And I asked Janice about that and she giggled and - - I said "It's sort of strange, isn't it, kid?" And she said, 'Well, he let me do that to him so that he could do what he wanted to do.' What he wanted to do, she never defined. Again, in my opinion, I think the child was a victim of incest, and I've always thought so, from the first time I ever met her."

When asked about her truancy in school, Marvin stated that Janice missed approximately 25-40 school days a year. She was an average student up until Mr. Adcock passed away and then things seem to go downhill quickly.

Wanda Holstein, the Unit Director in the Bartow County Juvenile Court, was called to the stand after Mr. Dickerson. She was a Court Service Worker when she first encountered Janice. Janice had been labeled a Status Offender and not a

Juvenile Delinquent. A Juvenile Delinquent was a child who had committed an offense that would normally be considered a crime and if they had committed the crime after his/her seventeenth birthday. A Status Offender was a child who commits those offenses that are limited to under the age of seventeen and are things such as being a truant or an unruly child.

Mrs. Holstein stated that a petition had been filed that alleged Janice was a deprived child. A deprived child is one whose parent or guardian is not meeting their basic needs of providing food, clothing, shelter, medical care, and education. Janice was found to be deprived and placed in the custody of the Department of Family and Children's Services.

According to Mrs. Holstein, Janice returned home to Elizabeth Adcock but conflict quickly developed between the two. Janice married Danny Buttrum shortly after returning home and because of that, she could no longer be charged with being a runaway or considered unruly by her parent. Janice had been reporting to Mrs. Holstein 1-2 times a week at that point, but contact with Janice ended in the summer of 1978. Mrs. Holstein visited Mrs. Adcock's home at that time. Mrs. Adcock was living in a camper type, one bedroom trailer in a trailer park called Cassville. The trailer was very dirty and Mrs. Holstein could smell the odor of alcohol on Mrs. Adcock's breath.

Mrs. Holstein described her interactions with Janice. She described Janice as being very immature for her age as well as, being quite impulsive. Wanda further stated that Janice appeared to look at the present and did not consider the consequences of the future. She also noted that Mrs. Adcock had never visited Janice while she was in the various foster facilities nor had she written any letters to her. Janice justified this by saying that it was hard for Mrs. Adcock to get to the post office, yet she lived approximately 1000 yards from the local post office and went there every month to get her VA check.

Mrs. Holstein maintained contact with Janice even after they closed her case in the summer of 1978. Janice called her when she became pregnant with her first child and again when the child was born. Her last phone call to Mrs. Holstein was just one week prior to the murder. Mrs. Holstein had been allowed to talk to Janice the night prior to her testifying in court. Afterwards, she commented that Janice seemed to understand the facts of what had occurred, but she was unsure if Janice understood the consequences. Mrs. Holstein felt that Janice had tunnel vision. She felt she had told the authorities what they needed and she was looking forward to going home. This was a typical reaction for an adolescent.

The next person called to the stand was Glenda Vaughn, a Casework Supervisor with the Bartow County Department of Family and Children Services. She had been in this position since September, 1973. Janice came to Glenda in October, 1976, and at this time she stated that she wished to be placed in a foster home. This led to Mrs. Vaughn visiting the Adcock home after her interview with Janice. She described the camper home as having food and dirty dishes scattered around the floor. There was a box overflowing with empty beer cans and boxes sat next to the door. There were also empty beer cans and bottles in the kitchen area of the camper.

Mrs. Vaughn further stated that, in her opinion, Janice had no one to model her behavior after. She was very immature for her age. Mrs. Vaughn also spoke with Janice the night before her testimony in court. She stated that she felt Janice understood where she was, but she didn't think Janice had any concept of what the future held for her. Glenda perceived Janice's maturity level as being between ten and thirteen years old.

With the conclusion of Mrs. Vaughn's testimony, the defense rested their case. District Attorney Steve Williams then began the task of bringing witnesses to the stand who would demonstrate that Janice was competent to stand trial. The first person he called to the stand was Dr. Timothy Bullard, a clinical psychologist with the Northwest Regional Hospital. He had been with this hospital for three years and his services were used to determine if a patient/defendant was competent to stand trial.

The first time that Dr. Bullard interacted with Janice was at the Whitfield County Correctional Center on October 27, 1980. There were two other people present during this interview. The first one was Dr. Kim, a psychiatrist, and a secretary, who was there to take notes. After his initial examination of Janice, Dr. Bullard noted some blocking and evasiveness. He described blocking as a subconscious process in which people will sometimes ignore or else forget things that are unpleasant to them. For example, a man might forget the date his wife died or the kind of car someone was driving that caused an accident. When Janice was asked questions, she would sometimes answer, "I really don't want to talk about it." After interviewing her, Dr. Bullard felt that she was competent to stand trial. Dr. Bullard testified that the most recent conversation he had with Janice was just a week before this trial. Mr. Fain objected on the grounds that he was unaware this particular conversation had ever taken place. However, Judge Pannell overruled the objection. Bullard testified there was no change in Janice's demeanor since his conversation with her in October. His first conversation with Janice lasted approximately one hour.

Dr. Bullard was asked how he would describe Janice on

a scale from minimum to maximum. He said that she was of average intelligence and not psychotic. On a scale from one to ten with five being minimum competency, he stated that Janice was above a five and probably closer to a six or seven. He thought that because of her unsophisticated vocabulary she might have a hard time understanding all of the legal terms used during the court proceedings. He did say that she would better understand things if it were expressed in a language that she could comprehend.

Dr. Bullard went on to state that after his initial interview with Janice that he wrote a letter to DA Williams. In that letter, he indicated that further psychological testing and evaluation may be necessary in order to determine competency. He did end by stating that to be totally fair to Janice that they had to look every possibility before a judgment on competency could be rendered.

Martha Glenn and Elizabeth Manis were each called to the stand. Both of these individuals were employed with the Whitfield County Sheriff's office during Janice's incarceration, and they had interacted with Janice at the jail. Martha and Elizabeth were employed as cooks and dealt with her during meal times and recreation. Both women stated that Janice was always well-mannered when dealing with them and that she was not a demanding inmate.

Juan A. Perez, a psychologist at Central State Hospital, was one of the professionals who had examined Janice during her 60-day stay at the same facility. Mr. Perez testified that he felt that Janice was capable of understanding the court proceedings and assisting her attorneys in her defense.

At this point, the judge sent the jury out for their evening meal. He asked that they freshen up and return to the jury box around 7:30 p.m. He wanted them to hear closing arguments and then they would be ready to deliberate after his instructions the next morning. None of the jurors objected to this when asked by the judge if this was okay.

DA Williams was the first one to give his closing argument. He reminded the jury that they were not there to determine the guilt or innocence of Janice Buttrum but to determine whether or not she was competent to stand trial. He reminded the jurors that seven people had testified on behalf of Janice. The first four people had contact with Janice prior to the murder, and they did not seem to have an opinion as to her competency. The other witnesses were experts in their respective fields and felt that Janice was competent.

Mr. Fain then addressed the jury. He stressed to the twelve men and women the deplorable circumstances surrounding Janice's childhood. Mr. Fain then asked them if they thought that these conditions could have an effect on an individual. He felt that Janice was looking for acceptance and that she told people what she thought they wanted to hear.

Mr. Fain described how the actions of Janice's parents had affected her. "Ladies and Gentlemen, I am contending to you that Mr. and Mrs. Adcock, probably out of ignorance, probably because they did not know how to do these things, affected Janice Buttrum's ability to cope with this world, affected her ability to communicate with me today, affected her ability to understand the nature and the object of these proceedings going on around her, as surely as if they had taken out a hammer and struck her on the head with it."

The jury was dismissed for the night. The judge told them that he would be disconnected the phones in each room but would allow the TV's to stay connected only if the jurors would not watch in news broadcasts. The jury was brought back the next morning to decide Janice's competency. After the jury had reached a verdict, Bennie Frost, the foreman of the jury passed the results to Judge Pannell. On February 6, 1981, the jury found Janice Marie Buttrum competent to stand trial.

Car belonging to Demetra Faye Parker

Exterior view of the Country Boy Inn

Exterior view of rooms at the Country Boy Inn

Exterior view of the office of the Country Boy Inn

Interior view of a room at the Country Boy Inn

Interior view of a room at the Country Boy Inn

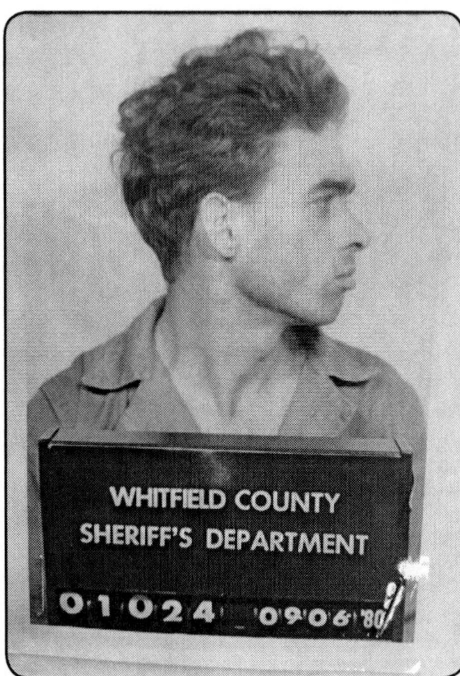

Mug Shot Danny Buttrum

Mug shot Janice Buttrum

Demetra Faye Parker

The author with Janice Buttrum - 2017

Chapter 14

Danny was represented by Mr. Greg Melton and Mr. Greg Brown in his competency trial. Before Melton began his opening remarks, he rolled a chalkboard in front of the jury. He explained to the jury that he would be using this outline to illustrate defense points throughout the trial. He joked that he was a Georgia Tech graduate and couldn't vouch for his spelling.

The first person called to the stand was Dr. Rodrigo Bonfante, a neurologist at Central State Hospital. He stated that he had examined Danny Buttrum and that Danny had described having headaches for the past four years. For three of those four years, he described having "spells". He suggested that these episodes caused him to lose his mind and sometimes caused him to become aggressive and destructive. He stated that on one of these occasions he had even threatened and injured his mother and, on several occasions, his wife Janice. Danny described a history of heavy alcohol and drug abuse but said that the "spells" occurred even when he was not under the influence. The patient also stated he had experienced visual and auditory hallucinations.

Dr. Bonfante felt that Danny appeared to be mildly retarded. He performed two separate EEG's on Mr. Buttrum, and both of these were abnormal. The doctor felt this could be from one of two things, epileptic problems or drug induced, but further testing was needed. He was leaning more toward drug induced. On cross examination, Mr. Williams suggested that Danny could possibly be "faking" and questioned the validity of Mr. Buttrum's drug use. Dr. Bonfante stated he had seen no documentation to verify the history that Mr. Buttrum had given.

The jury recessed for lunch after the Dr.'s testimony. Upon their return, Mr. Ray Swanson took the stand. Ray was a deputy sheriff for Whitfield County and testified to a report that was made regarding Danny inflicting scratches on his wrist with a broken ballpoint pen. He was taken to the hospital for treatment and put back in isolation. Mr. Swanson described Danny as requiring more close attention than the other inmates. He stated that he had never personally interacted with Danny.

Evelyn Buttrum, the mother of Danny Buttrum, stated that Danny had been approximately fourteen-years-old when he began drinking and this increased to a heavier consumption when he was sixteen-years- old. This heavy usage had been ongoing for approximately fourteen years. She stated that he drank every weekend to the point of intoxication. At one time, Danny was ordered to the Coosa Valley Mental Health Center for evaluation. This was after he had ripped the telephone from the wall and broken windows in Mrs. Buttrum's home.

Mrs. Buttrum had confirmed Danny's history of violence. She verified that he had "spells" and that during these spells that he became violent and would have not any memory of his violent outbursts. Evelyn was asked if Danny had ever had any head injuries. She testified that three to four years prior to this, Danny had been struck in the head with a hammer, but this had occurred after the violent spells had started taking place.

After Danny had spent two to three weeks at Coosa Valley, Evelyn stated that he had returned to her residence and attempted to overdose on Valium on that same day. Two weeks after that, he attempted to overdose again with pills belonging to Evelyn and another son. She had been visiting with Danny on a weekly basis since his incarceration. She adamantly felt that Danny was incapable of assisting his attorneys.

Mr. Brown asked Evelyn about her own education experience and she stated that she had completed the second grade. According to Evelyn, Danny's father passed away approximately ten years ago and he had previously been treated at Milledgeville.

Inez White, a neighbor and best friend of Evelyn, confirmed Evelyn's previous testimony regarding Danny's mental health issues. She stated that she and Evelyn had been close friends for approximately ten years and she would do anything to help her. She also stated that she had not seen or spoken to Danny in approximately ten months.

Danny's older brother Larry testified that he had seen Danny use a variety of drugs including marijuana, speed, downers, and acid. According to Larry, Danny had used these drugs many times but never in the presence of their mother. He also acknowledged that Danny had been a heavy drinker since age sixteen and had mixed alcohol with a variety of drugs. Larry only visited Danny once in jail and that was the day before he was to testify in court. Prior to that, Danny had gone to his brother's house two weeks before he and Janice were arrested in Florida.

Reid Hobson was brought in to testify about Danny's school record. Permanent records indicated that Danny quit school at age sixteen. Early records indicated that he had failed first, fourth, fifth and sixth grades. It was noted that fifty percent of the grades that were listed were failing. When

Danny quit school at the age of sixteen, he was in the 7th grade. It was suggested he had been socially promoted on several occasions and was three to four years older than his peers. Records showed he had repeated grades 5 and 6.

Jesse Collette testified that he had interacted with Danny when he was a resident at the Rome Mental Health Center in 1977. When Danny arrived at the center, he expressed to Mr. Collette that he was having sex problems. He was preoccupied with sex and was having hostile feelings toward his mother. Danny also described having paranoid feelings and hallucinations. Part of these hallucinations were of someone molesting him and emasculating him. Danny also appeared disoriented. When asked what month it was, Danny stated that it was January instead of July. Mr. Collette felt that Danny was exhibiting symptoms of schizophrenia. He testified that he had spent approximately one hour with Danny for this evaluation. Danny was then admitted to the Adult Psych Unit. Mr. Collette stated that he had not seen Danny since that time. On cross examination, Mr. Collette admitted to DA Williams that he did remember the interactions that he had with Danny. One other witness, Mr. Lively, verified the information presented by Mr. Collette.

After Mr. Lively's testimony, there was a brief recess before the next witness was called. John Parker, a jailer with the Whitfield County Sheriff's Department, explained the daily routine of what happens at the jail. Mr. Parker described his interactions with Danny Buttrum at the jail. He stated that Danny was able to participate in the daily activities without any difficulties. Mr. Parker did feel that Danny was competent to stand trial.

Hugh Don Smith, the confidential informant that had been placed with Danny was called to the stand. Mr. Smith testified that he was currently incarcerated at the Federal Correctional Institute in Sandstone, Minnesota. Previously, he was at the Whitfield County Jail while he was attending a court hearing at the District Court in Rome. He was there for a period of four to five days. Hugh Don interacted with Danny and they discussed Danny's court proceedings.

Danny had discussed his previous suicide attempt with Hugh Don. After this attempt, Danny was placed in an isolated cell at night. He was becoming frustrated with his arrangement of being moved from cell to cell. Hugh Don tried to explain to Danny that this was normal since Danny had tried to harm himself. Danny replied to Hugh Don, "Well, I wished I hadn't done that. I was just doing that to try to play crazy." He indicated that he wished that the sheriff knew that so he would be left alone. Hugh Don conveyed this information, and Danny was left in one cell after promising not to harm himself.

Mr. Smith's previous criminal history and the possibility of his being untruthful was brought in to question by Mr. Melton, Danny's attorney. Hugh Don admitted to the fact that he had been used as a criminal informant before. Most recently he had worked with the ATF and U.S. Attorney's office regarding a plot to murder a DA in neighboring Floyd County. When asked if he had received monetary compensation, Hugh Don replied that he had not. He stated that he performed the services quid pro quo, which is Latin "something for something." On cross, DA Williams asked Mr. Smith if they had a deal with each other regarding Mr. Smith's services and Hugh Don replied "No."

Dr. Timothy Bullard and Dr. Lower from Central State both testified that they did not find Danny to be mentally retarded. It was thought that there could be a possibility that Danny was malingering or possibly faking his condition. These were the last two witnesses of the day. The jury was recessed until the next day.

The following morning, closing arguments were made by both attorneys. DA Williams implied that Danny's issues could have been brought on by his use of illicit substances. After deliberation, the jury found that Danny was competent to stand trial for the murder of Demetra Parker.

Chapter 15

To avoid repetition of information, the testimonies given in the case of Danny Buttrum are greatly abbreviated unless the testimony given is different than that given in Janice Buttrum's case.

Originally, Danny and Janice wanted to be tried together. However, Judge Pannell quickly ruled that the pair would be tried separately since they had each been indicted by the grand jury. Mr. Fain wanted to get Janice tried first. He thought that, due to her pregnancy and age, this might gain her some favor with a jury when it came to the death penalty. However, her obstetrician decided that the trial might be too stressful for the young mother.

Danny's trial began on March 9, 1981. He was being charged with murder, rape, and theft by taking. Greg Melton was one of the defense attorneys and was quick to explain to the jurors that death in the electric chair was on the table.

A series of GBI and FBI agents testified about the murder scene at the Country Boy Inn and the ultimate arrest of Danny and Janice. FBI Agent Cowgill stated that Danny had told him he had found the 1975 Buick with the keys in the ignition in the hotel parking lot. Danny and Janice had decided to escape in that same car. Agents also testified that when Danny was arrested he did not appear to be under the influence of drugs or alcohol. Danny at first denied knowing Demetra Parker or having anything to do with her murder.

Mr. Cowgill explained Danny's version of the night's events. Danny and his wife, Janice Buttrum, had met the victim, Demetra Parker, at the Country Boy Inn approximately two or three days prior to her death. He stated that on the day of Demetra's death, he and his wife had devised a plan to get her to open her door to them. Janice would knock on the door and request a cigarette. He stated that they proceeded to her room and knocked on the door. Janice was holding the child in her arms when Demetra opened the door. After Janice asked for a cigarette, Danny pushed open the door and they all went in. He recounted how Janice placed the baby on the floor, turned the light on, and closed the door. He described grabbing Demetra and wrestling her to the floor. He stated that Janice removed a three-inch pocket knife from his right front pants pocket and stabbed Demetra several times in the upper chest and heart area. At this time, he explained his wife gave him the knife, and he proceeded to stab Demetra several times. Danny then admitted to raping Demetra. Afterward, he got up, went to the sink, and washed off the blood. When he turned around, his wife was stabbing Demetra. She gave the knife back to him and he stabbed Demetra several more times. He then inserted a plastic cylinder-shaped object into her vagina.

Dr. James Metcalfe concluded the first day's testimony. He testified to the horrific damage that had been done to Demetra. She suffered approximately 97 stab wounds with the majority of them located in the left upper chest area around the heart. It was his opinion that Demetra was alive during all of these wounds until just prior to the final gashing wound made across her abdomen. He also testified that there were no defense wounds present on Demetra's body.

At the end of the first day's testimony, Judge Pannell gave

instructions to the jurors, who were being sequestered for the duration of the trial. Each juror would be given his/her own room. Judge Pannell stated that the rooms would all be side by side so that no doors faced each other. He did allow the jurors to keep the televisions in their rooms to help occupy their time at night, but he removed the telephones. Both a male bailiff and a female assistance would be on hand to address any emergencies that might occur during the night. The group would dine together each night at the Oakwood Café and then spend the nights at the Holiday Inn. The first day of court ended at 5:45 in the afternoon.

Judge Pannell addressed the jury the next morning to make sure there were no concerns from the night before. He asked them if there was anything he could do to make their stay a more pleasant experience. One female juror, Ms. Saltzman, was quick to reply bring her husband. The judge apologized for not being able to fulfill her request.

Day Two of testimony began at 9:45 a.m. with evidence presented by Connie Pickens and John Wegel, from the State Crime Lab, who testified about the blood found at the crime scene. Although DNA was an unheard of concept, the technicians were able to type the blood. It was found to be type O, which at the time was found in 45% of the population.

Timothy Sexton was called to the stand. He identified Danny as the man he saw walking by the door to Demetra's room 15-20 times on the night of September 2. He had been there with his friend Donald Goforth. The pair, along with Demetra, had bought beer and settled in Demetra's room to watch the news and "The Rookies." Donald stated that he got up and shut the door on Demetra's request because she said that Danny scared her. Timothy testified that he had not met or interacted with Danny prior to his appearance in court that day. However, Donald had seen Danny on one prior trip to the Country Boy Inn but had not interacted him.

Richard Dunnigan confirmed the timeline of the murder with his testimony. Demetra's room backed up to his at the hotel. Around 4:00 a.m. on the morning of September 3, he awoke to the sound of a baby crying. He claimed to hear no other sounds and went back to sleep.

Christopher Lee "Leon" Busby stated that on the afternoon of September 2, he first made the acquaintance of Danny Buttrum. Danny interrupted a conversation that Leon was having with the maid. Leon allowed Danny and Janice to borrow his blue Gran Torino that evening to go riding around. The pair did not return his car until around 3:45 a.m. on the morning of September 3rd.

Sybil Rogers and Dorothy Chastain both testified to interacting with Danny on the evening of September 2 and how he had attempted to lure both women from their homes. Both stated they felt that Danny was possibly under the influence of alcohol and Dorothy even said that he was acting "wild" which was completely out of character for him.

FBI Agent Fred McFaul also spoke about the confession that he had heard from Danny Buttrum. He stated that Danny had told him that he and Janice had gone to their friend Demetra's room under the guise of getting a cigarette. Janice knocked on the door and when Demetra answered, Danny pushed the door open and attacked Demetra physically. He thought that Janice closed the door and turned on the light. Danny said that he forced Demetra on her back and pinned her arms to the floor with his hands. He claimed that Janice reached into his right front pocket, removed a pocket knife, and began stabbing Demetra. After stabbing her several times, Janice handed the knife to Danny and he also stabbed

Demetra. He stated that Demetra was screaming and struggling. Danny also admitted to raping Demetra and after getting up to wash his hands, Janice began stabbing Demetra again. He then returned and stabbed Demetra several more times before inserting a plastic object in her vagina.

It was now time for the confidential informant, Hugh Don Smith, to take the stand. Previous testimony had indicated Hugh Don was being housed in the Whitfield County Jail while attending federal hearings in Rome. During that time, Smith was granted trustee status in the jail which allowed him to be out of his cell during daylight hours and returned to his cell around 6:00 p.m. each evening. Due to his mechanical experience he was allowed to work on officers' patrol cars. Hugh Don had supposedly volunteered his services to spend time with Danny to gain information.

Hugh Don had been used as a paid confidential government informant on approximately twenty-five other occasions. He had done this to receive a reduction in the federal prison time that he was serving. Mr. Melton was against Hugh Don testifying and stated it was a violation of Danny's rights since he already had an attorney. However, Whitfield County officials denied having had any such agreement with Mr. Smith; Still, a letter had been sent to the federal prison in Minnesota where Smith was housed, regarding the reason for Mr. Smith's return to Dalton to testify in the case of Danny Buttrum. Sheriff Davis testified on the stand that he did not know that Smith had been used as a CI in the past.

Mr. Melton asked Hugh Don if he had ever lied under oath. He admitted that he had. He stated, "The truth only matters if my butt is in a sling." Hugh Don claimed that he told Danny to keep his mouth shut and listen to his attorney. Danny would spend the days in Hugh Don's cell and at night he would be placed in a single-man security cell. When Danny expressed his frustration with the situation, Hugh Don explained it was because Danny had tried to hurt himself. Danny confided to Hugh Don that his actions were all part of his plan to "play crazy."

Danny related his version of the facts in the case to Hugh Don. He stated he was jealous of Janice spending time with Demetra and he thought there was the possibility that they were having sexual relations. He said that he pressured his wife into proving to him that she loved him by going to the room with him and committing numerous offenses against the young lady.

Larry Buttrum again testified on his brother's behalf. He stated that Danny had been a heavy drinker since beginning to drink moonshine at age 15. Danny was 29 years old now, so he had been drinking almost half of his life. He had begun taking speed at age 14 and later escalated to marijuana and LSD. Danny did not do drugs and alcohol around his mother, but he did seem to have trouble following her rules. He also had a very sporadic work history.

For the first time, a woman named Patricia Spivey appeared to testify. She had seen Danny and Janice on the night of September 2, 1980. They were with Leon Busby between the hours of 11 p.m. and midnight at a trailer on Mill Creek Road. Both Danny and Leon had been drinking. They later came by to see if Ann Ray would go with them. They stayed approximately 30-45 min. Patricia stated that she and her children had been living with Buford Phillips at the time. Buford had drunk a few beers with Danny and Leon while they were in Leon's Gran Torino. Buford backed up Patricia's testimony.

Bobby Chandler had also been visited by Janice and Danny on the night of September 2. He was living in Adairsville and had been a classmate of Danny's. Bobby testified that Danny had been drinking heavily over the past few years and could easily drink a case of beer at a time. The couple, along with their baby, came to Bobby's house between midnight and 1:00 a.m. By that point, Danny had already drunk 12-15 beers and seemed to be high. Bobby stated that his eyes were red and he was staggering. Danny had explained to Bobby that he was "on the run" from the work camp.

Dr. Ilhan Ermutlu, who had previously completed a mental health examination on Danny, was called to testify. His notes revealed an interview with Danny's mother Evelyn. Those notes stated that Danny had been dropped on his head as a baby and that his head had struck the floor. Approximately four years ago, Danny had been struck in the head with a hammer, but he did not seek medical attention for this injury. According to his mother, he was briefly unconscious and after that he began to experience headaches. He also stated that Danny had a serious drinking problem. The doctor felt that Danny could possibly have pathological intoxication. This means a person has an allergy to alcohol. The person will respond with a drastic change in personality and behavior. They react violently with or without provocation, and they don't remember what happens afterwards. However, after reading all the notes concerning Danny and the events surrounding September 3, Dr. Ermutlu did not feel that he could confidently make this a definitive diagnosis.

The doctor also testified that Danny had violent thoughts. Danny had expressed his thoughts about killing people, killing his mother, and his wife, and raping people. He had also attempted suicide several times in the past. Dr. Ermutlu was asked if Danny's excessive drinking could have brought on the events of September 3, and he replied that he did not think it did. Later, he was asked about the results of the Minnesota Multiphasic Personality Inventory for Danny. He stated that the psychologist felt that Danny's "F" scale was high. This is a fake scale especially when people are wanting to show themselves to be sicker than what they are. They do this by marking more of the pathological statements on the test. He agreed with DA Williams that Danny was probably trying to present himself in the worse possible light.

When asked if he thought Danny could possibly suffer from Antisocial Personality, the doctor replied that would almost be too much of a compliment to Danny. He went on to say that a typical Antisocial Personality individual can manipulate their environment rather successfully. However, one of the things to disprove this diagnosis was Danny's suicide attempts. He stated that one rarely sees suicide attempts an Antisocial Personality because they like themselves too much to do harm to themselves. On redirect, Mr. Melton showed that nowhere in those notes was Danny ever diagnosed as being a sociopath.

Danny did not testify on his own behalf. It took less than an hour for the jury to find Danny guilty on all counts.

Chapter 16

The sentencing phase began the next day to determine if Danny would be sentenced to the electric chair. The purpose of the sentencing phase is to bring in witnesses to testify to the character of the person who has been found guilty. (The author felt that it was important to include this information regarding Danny in order for the reader to gain a better look at both defendants in the case.)

The first person called in Danny's sentencing phase was Captain Don Marler, the warden of the Cobb County work camp. Captain Marler testified that Danny came to the work camp on July 14th, 1980 because he had violated the terms of his probation. He did not receive any special privileges while he was there. Danny escaped the work camp on August 9th, 1980. Captain Marler did not give any information regarding Danny's character, or if he thought Danny should receive leniency.

The next witness was Devon Crump and she testified about an incident that happened on November 22, 1975. Devon described meeting Danny when he pulled up in her yard on the premise of asking directions. She noted that she began to feel uncomfortable when Danny began asking her personal questions such as: Did she have a boyfriend and where were her parents. At this point, Devon told Danny she had to go and quickly retreated into her house. The situation escalated when Danny entered the home behind her, grabbed her forcibly by the arms, and pulled her to him. She struggled with him and finally pushed him away. On cross, Devon was asked if she met Danny before this incident, but she denied knowing Danny previously. She was then questioned about a previous report regarding this incident where Danny had said he would walk her to the door. She, however, did not remember this taking place.

Following Miss Crumps, testimony, Detective James Crisp testified that he had investigated the incident involving Danny and Miss Crump. At the time, he was an investigator with the Gordon County Sheriff's Department. He stated that he had administered the Miranda rights to Danny and then began questioning him about Miss Crump's claims. Danny admitted to leaving Smitty's bar around 5:00 p.m. after drinking heavily. He stopped at Miss Crump's house. According to Danny's story, he said he only asked for a drink of water and with her permission followed her in the house. He started to grab her then ran out of the house. For this incident, Danny was charged with simple battery.

Agent Charles Johnson of the GBI was called to the stand next and was asked about an interview with Danny on September 6, 1980. In this interview, Danny stated he didn't feel bad about killing Demetra, and he didn't feel he was wrong. Danny's statement was inconsistent with what he told the FBI. On cross examination Mr. Melton asked if this was the first time Danny's statements had been inconsistent and Johnson replied, "Yes."

Jesse Padgett Collette, a senior counselor at the Department of Offender Rehabilitation in Rome, saw Danny in July, 1977, at a crisis intervention session. The facility was the Rome Diversion Center and was a residential treatment program for young men on probation. She testified that Danny voluntarily came to the center because of his preoccupation with sex and rape. Mr. Collette explained that Danny's mother was with him at the time of this meeting and stated that recently Danny had threatened her with a butcher knife and scissors. This attack had occurred two weeks prior to this meeting with Mr. Collette.

Mamie Buttrum Shope, Danny's half-sister was called next. She and Danny had the same father, although Mamie was at least 40 years older than her half-brother. She testified that there was approximately a thirty-year difference between Evelyn Buttrum and Danny's father. Mamie was asked if their father had ever been hospitalized for mental problems, and she admitted that he had been a patient in Milledgeville in 1967. The senior Mr. Buttrum also had two sisters and a brother who had died there. One sibling had been a patient there for over thirty years. Danny's grandfather was also a patient at Milledgeville. Mr. Williams asked her if any of them had ever committed murder and she said "No."

The former chief of police of Adairsville, Mr. Bob Jamison, who was currently with the DA's office in Bartow County, stated he had previously met Danny when he was an inmate at the Cherokee County Work Camp. He presented a copy of Danny's criminal record which detailed multiple arrests for drug related offenses. As for his perception of Danny, he stated that Danny could be deceiving to those who did not know him and regarded him as somewhat reckless.

Dr. Metcalfe who had performed the autopsy on Demetra testified as to the condition of the body. He stated he could find no evidence of forcible oral sodomy but couldn't rule it out. There had been some degree of bruising on the lips and he couldn't rule out oral sex. On cross, DA Williams asked Dr. Metcalfe if he had ever seen a rape-murder of this magnitude and he replied "No."

Harold Dale, the mayor of Adairsville from 1976-1979, had known Danny his entire life. He testified that he was involved with Danny mainly through Boy Scouts. He believed Danny was in his teens when he lost his father. During the four years he was mayor, Danny appeared before him six times during traffic court. Five of these offenses were alcohol related. Mr. Dale allowed Danny to work for the city maintenance crew to help him with some of his fines. He stated that Danny often became violent when he drank and that he also had problems holding down a job. On cross examination, DA Williams asked Mr. Dale about a conversation that he had had with Danny a few months prior to the murder. He talked with Danny for approximately 20 minutes and told him that if he didn't quit drinking and taking dope that something bad was going to happen to him.

Danny's mother Evelyn testified that he had three brothers and five half-sisters and that he was the youngest child. She explained again how her son had quit school at 16 and started taking drugs at 14. He was first given pills by a lady who had hired him to catch chickens. This job sometimes required Danny to work all night and then he would struggle to go to school the next day. Around this same time (1967), Danny's parents separated and Mr. Buttrum passed away just three years later. She admitted to knowing that he had been a heavy drinker for the past fourteen years.

Evelyn also testified that Danny had asked to be taken to the mental hospital in Rome in 1977. She explained that Danny had tried to commit suicide on two prior occasions by overdosing on pills. She claimed to have seen Danny and Janice on a daily basis and noted that when Danny was drinking that Janice seemed to be able to control him. On cross, Evelyn admitted to DA Williams that she had witnessed Danny demonstrating violent behavior even when he wasn't drinking. She wanted the court to know that although Danny had threatened to strike her, he had never followed through on these threats.

Mrs. Buttrum then asked for the opportunity to address the jury. She stated, "I am sorry that he did this. I don't know what else to say. I wish it hadn't happened. If I could do - - if I could bring the girl back, I would I sure am sorry."

Dr. Joel Norris was brought to the stand in order to help the jury better understand "unconscious motivation." He had spent approximately twelve hours interviewing Danny, another two hours with Evelyn, and one with Janice. He related to the court that Danny did well when he was in a more structured environment. It was his opinion that Danny and Janice had formed a symbiotic relationship, one in which they were feeding off each other's positive aspects, as well as negative aspects. He also mentioned that Danny had blamed his mother for his father's death.

Dr. Norris reflected on a classic case involving the Kalikak family. This was a family from a book entitled "*The Kalikak Family – A Study in the Heredity of Feeble Mindedness*" written by the American psychologist Henry Goddard in 1912. The book was based on a case study on feeble mindedness and incorporated such things as mental retardation, learning disabilities, and mental illness. His thoughts were that many of these traits were hereditary, and therefore people having such traits should be limited in reproducing offspring. In this story, these people were referred to as "poor protoplasm" or bad stock.

Dr. Norris stated, "When you are born into such a situation, you tend to feel entrapped, imprisoned in that lifestyle, and somehow feel that you never will be able to get out of it." His explanation was that it is bred from one generation to the next. He claimed that Danny bordered on mental retardation and that he suffered from a lack of ego development. Dr. Norris described Sigmund Freud's three parts of ego development: id, ego and super ego. Id is primitive like a child sucking a nipple or a pubescent wanting to have sex. The super ego is what we learn from church, our parents, and what is right and wrong. The ego acts as a mediator between these two areas. Dr. Norris stated that Danny had almost no ego, and was willing to go along with the crowd. He also noted that Danny had asked for help with his urges and his headaches, but he didn't have the ability within himself to follow through.

Dr. Norris claimed that Janice, in his opinion, was smarter than Danny and that she could be very manipulative. He stated that he thought Janice was perhaps the one "calling the shots." Dr. Norris felt that Janice was dominant and very jealous, and that Danny probably didn't realize he was being manipulated by Janice. On cross, Dr. Norris admitted he worked with a group that was opposed to capital punishment and he was aware that Danny's sentence involved the possibility of capital punishment.

Next to testify was Dr. Timothy Bullard, the Director of Forensic Services at Northwest Georgia Regional Hospital in Rome. He again testified about Danny's extensive history of alcohol and amphetamine abuse. The defense had tried to imply that Danny possibly suffered from organic delusional syndrome vs schizophrenic reaction. Dr. Bullard had not examined Danny in 1977 nor had he later. There were also no drug tests performed on Danny. On cross, the DA implied that organic brain syndrome had an etiology of possible alcohol withdrawal, delirium, or dementia. DA Williams suggested that if Danny was off the stimulants that he could control his behavior. Dr. Bullard said he was unsure if he agreed with this because he had only seen Danny while he was off drugs.

In closing arguments, DA Williams related that he thought that the letter from Janice stating that she took all the blame was deceptive. He felt that if she truly meant her confession, she would have been there to exonerate her husband. (Janice stated to the author that she was approached with the possibility of a plea deal at some point prior to trial. As part of the deal, she would agree to testify against Danny. However, Janice did not agree with all of the terms of the deal and turned it down.) Mr. Williams adamantly told the court that Danny was a pervert and a coward as was guilty of murder, rape, and car theft, and the verdict should be death. He said "Can you say that Demetra Parker suffered any less a fate than the Christians did from the claws and the jaws of those lions?" He went on to say, "Give Mercy to Ray Parker, for he has suffered and his suffering continue. Give him peace." In his final statement, he declared, "We will not tolerate savages acting like cannibals, butchering and raping innocent teenage girls."

Greg Melton argued for the life of Danny Buttrum. He stated, "I am no rock, I am not insensitive. I am not unsympathetic. I am an advocate." He too brought up Janice's letter and used it to show that Danny did not consciously seek out Demetra or plan her demise without Janice's involvement. He described Danny using the words of Dr. Norris, "Danny Buttrum, the person, is poor protoplasm. He's rotten stock." He went on to describe Janice as "the conniving, manipulative one; she instigated these dominoes before they fell. She was the first domino."

It took the jury merely forty-two minutes to sentence Danny Buttrum to the electric chair.

Chapter 17

The criminal trial of the State of Georgia vs Janice Buttrum began on Friday, August 28, 1981. The trial had been delayed due to Janice's pregnancy with her second child. Once the child was born, she was placed in the custody of Danny Buttrum's brother and sister-in-law. Janice's foster mother Elizabeth Adcock had basically cut all ties with Janice at this point. Janice sat there at the defense table all alone in her ill-fitting clothes with no family members behind her to offer moral support.

DA Williams began by describing to the jury that Janice was being charged with murder in the death of Demetra Parker and theft by taking in regard to Demetra's car being taken by the Buttrums. The testimonies began with information given by GBI Agents Johnson and Dodd, as well as FBI Agent McFaul. They each were called on to describe the crime scene found at the Country Boy Inn, the photos taken, and also information gained from Evelyn Buttrum that eventually led to the arrest of Janice and Danny in Pensacola.

On cross examination of Agent McFaul, he stated that the arresting officer had placed her in his car and returned her to the local FBI office. Agent McFaul described coming into contact with a knife in the defendant's car. Agent McFaul drove the car with Janice's baby Alexis inside to his office. As he was exiting the vehicle, he leaned over to retrieve Alexis from the car and carry her into the office. At this time, he saw a pocketbook on the passenger floor of the vehicle, and a knife handle protruding from that pocketbook. Agent McFaul did not recover the knife. He stated that he secured the vehicle at the Police Department and assumed that Whitfield County authorities and the GBI Agent took possession of it next. On redirect, Agent McFaul described the knife to DA Williams as a straight blade knife, not a folding knife.

Author Note: There was no knife that was entered into evidence. There has been a conflict as to whether both Demetra and Danny had knives or just Danny. Local officials and Danny claimed that a knife was thrown from the car into the highway median after the couple left Dalton. However local officials searched the area described by Danny and no knife was ever found.

On the second morning of the trial, Mr. Fain started by expressing his concern about media coverage of the trial and the possibility that the sequestered jury could have been exposed to both the commercial previews and the actual broadcasts. Judge Pannell asked each of the jurors whether they were able to avoid the news from the previous evening at the hours of 6 p.m., 7 p.m. and 11 p.m. All of the jurors denied having watched any of the broadcasts.

As the trial proceeded, Dr. Metcalfe, a forensic pathologist, testified about the autopsy he had performed on Demetra Parker. There was a total of 97 stab wounds found on the body. Sixty-seven stab wounds were found in the left chest area of the body. He went on to say that there signs of blunt force trauma to the head and face area. Her body showed no signs of defensive wounds. Demetra also showed signs of being raped vaginally and rectally.

Connie Pickens, a Forensic Serologist with the Georgia State Crime Laboratory, described the blood stains that were submitted to her lab. (Just a reminder that this is prior to the use of DNA and the only thing that could be determined was blood type.) Both blood stains and a bloody washcloth found at the scene were found to contain blood type O. These were items that had been given to her by GBI Agent Johnson. Mrs. Pickens also examined a blue nightgown and panties. Neither of these items contained seminal fluid. Mrs. Pickens also explained that 45% of the general population has Blood Type O.

Henry Wallace took the stand to testify about his relationship with Demetra Parker, whom he had known for approximately four years. They had met in Dyersburg, TN and Demetra had been his girlfriend. When he was asked why she came to Dalton, he explained that she had wanted to be with him. Henry also stated that Demetra had decided that she wanted to go back home to Kenton. He also verified her ownership of a 1975 Buick, and on September 2, testified that he saw clothes in Demetra's car. DA Williams asked him if Demetra smoked Marlboro cigarettes and he said that she did not. On cross examination, Henry Wallace stated that Demetra had only been living in Dalton for about a month prior to September 2, 1980.

Next on the witness stand was Donald Goforth, a friend of Timmy Sexton and through this friendship, he had met Demetra. Donald identified the car Demetra was driving on September 2 and that she had picked him up, along with Timmy Sexton. The three friends had arrived at the Country Boy Inn around 6:15 p.m. They stayed in Demetra's room approximately 2 hours watched the news and the "Rookies." Donald then identified a photo of Danny Buttrum and stated that during that time he had walked past Demetra's door approximately twenty times. Donald stated that he finally jumped up and locked the door because Demetra stated that she was afraid of Danny. The trio left the room around 8:25 that night.

On cross examination, Donald testified that he had drunk a couple of beers when he was in Demetra's room. He stated he could not recall if Demetra or Timmy drank any beer but that the beer had been purchased from the local Golden Gallon store. Donald also admitted that he was not old enough to purchase the beer on his own and neither was his friend Tommy. Donald explained to Mr. Fain that he had not seen Janice Buttrum at any point while they were at the Country Boy Inn.

Timmy Sexton verified his friend's story that he had been with Donald and Demetra on the night of September 2. His testimony matched that of his friend Donald's timeline. He also testified to the fact that Danny Buttrum was pacing back and forth in front of the Demetra's door. Both young men agreed that when Demetra dropped them back at Timmy's house that she had no visible physical injuries.

Leon Busby, who also lived at the Country Boy Inn in September, 1980, was called to the stand. He spoke of meeting Danny and Janice Buttrum on September 2, 1980. The pair had met that morning when Danny interrupted a conversation that Leon was having with the maid at the inn. The two met up again around 3 p.m. to share a couple of beers together. This was a brief encounter lasting approximately twenty minutes. Around 6:30 that evening, Danny had approached Leon and asked him to take him across the interstate to purchase more beer. Janice and their baby accompanied the two men to the store. Leon claimed that Danny asked him where he could "get a girl at." Leon questioned whether or not Janice would be upset by this request. Danny had replied, "No, as long as she gets to go with her first." After this, the group traveled to two different truck stops and to both Sybil's and Dottie's houses. Except for the first stop where they all had something to drink, neither Janice nor Leon got out at any of the other stops.

Leon went on to testify that the group returned to the Country Boy Inn after the last stop. Danny asked to borrow Leon's car for approximately 3-4 hours. At first, Leon denied the request and stated that Danny could use the car for only 30 minutes and Danny agreed. However, Danny took Leon's car and did not return it for 3-4 hours. When Danny and Janice returned, Leon saw the car lights shining through the hotel window and went to the room door. The couple was on the balcony above him and told him they had left the keys underneath the floor mat of the car. Their room was directly above Leon's room. When asked if Danny and Janice had been drinking during the evening, Leon replied Danny had drunk over a half case of beer, but he had not seen Janice drink any. Leon stated the he had only drunk one beer the entire day.

On cross examination, Leon told Greg Brown that he had been living at the Country Boy Inn off and on for approximately five years. When he was asked how much he had had to drink that day, Leon again replied that he'd drank just one beer. He admitted that he usually drank more than that on a daily basis and was known to drink to excess on the weekend. He stated that he had only beer that day because he was recovering from a hangover. Leon repeated that he had met Danny Buttrum the morning of September 2 but did not meet Janice until that afternoon. He stated that Danny paid for the beer at the Golden Gallon, and then they had stopped at one truck stop for Danny to pick up a radio that he had left behind. Leon then admitted that they had gone to a residence on Haig Mill Road for the purpose of getting an address from a woman named Ann for the police in regards to some stolen guns.

Next, the trio went to the '66 truck stop, drank a cup of

coffee, and stayed for approximately ten minutes. While they were there, Danny spoke to someone about money that was owed to him. Leon seemed to think the man might have been the owner of the truck stop. They next went to the Amoco truck stop which was across the interstate, and there Danny called someone about a job.

Leon then described going to the Thomas Motel on South 41 to visit a woman named Sybil. He explained that Danny went to the door while Leon and Janice stayed in the car. From there they went to Dottie's apartment, and again Leon and Janice stayed in the car. This was between 10:00 and 10:30 p.m.

The next person called to testify was Sybil Rogers. She stated that she lived at the Peach State Motel and worked at the Amoco Truck Stop. She had seen Danny Buttrum at her work but had never met his wife, Janice. She did not consider Danny to be a friend. She stated that on September 2, she was at her home with her boyfriend Herschel Thomason. Around 11:30, there was a knock on the door and Sybil got up from the bed to answer the door. Surprised to see Danny, she had asked him how he had gotten her address and he informed her that a lady at the truck stop had told him. Danny then asked her if she would go outside with him so that he could speak to her in private. However, Herschel stepped up and replied to Danny, "No, what you've got to say, you say it in front of both of us." Danny apologized several times for interrupting and left their apartment. Sybil claimed to have seen a car belonging to Leon Busby and that Leon was in the driver seat. Sybil also described seeing a blonde-haired woman in the back seat. On cross examination, Sybil stated that she had been working part time at the truck stop and that is how she had met Danny Buttrum.

Dorothy Chastain testified that she also worked at the Phillips '66 truck stop and knew both Danny and Janice from living at the Country Boy Inn. Dorothy stated that she had seen Danny twice on the night of September 2 at her new apartment on Hwy 41 South. The first time was close to 6 p.m. when he came to her door for a brief conversation. Dorothy stated that she could tell that Danny had been drinking at the time. The second encounter occurred between 11:00 and 12:00. At that time, he was in Leon Busby's car, a black and white Torino. This time, she stated she could smell alcohol on Danny's breath. Dorothy said that she had a coffee pot on the stove, and it started whistling about the same time she answered the door. She stepped away to take the pot off the stove and when she turned around Danny was in the kitchen with her. Danny had reached for her, but she pushed his hands away. She told him that her landlord was very strict, and she wanted him to leave. Dorothy was afraid after this encounter, so she put on her clothes and went to the truck stop. As she passed Sybil Roger's home on her way there, she saw Leon's car parked there.

On cross examination, Dorothy stated that she had known Danny for approximately three months and considered him a friend. At the time of the first visit, Dorothy saw a man in the car with Danny and they were in a beige small car like a Datsun or Toyota. She stated that Danny had a beer in his hand. On the second visit, Dorothy had observed a man she knew as Leon Busby in the driver's seat and Janice Buttrum in the back seat.

Pam Henry, another resident of the Country Boy Inn, stated that her room was located behind Demetra Parker's. She stated that in the early morning hours of September 3, she awoke to someone pounding on her door. Rather than going to the door, she called maintenance and asked him to find out who was knocking on her door. He told her that it was probably someone with the wrong room or else was drunk. His response was to ignore the knocking and go back to sleep. Pam stated that she did not get up and look out the curtain. Nearly an hour later at 4 a.m., she claimed to have heard a woman screaming. On cross, Pam stated that it was not unusual to hear noises during the night due to the transient population at the hotel.

Danny's employer, Mr. John Teems, the owner of the Phillip '66 truck stop, was called to the stand next. Danny had worked for him on three separate occasions. He knew that Danny and Janice were living at the Country Boy Inn, and that they did not have an automobile. Danny relied on friends for transportation back and forth to work. Mr. Teems claimed to have seen Danny on the evening of September 2 at the truck stop. He testified that Danny was driving what he thought was a Buick, but he did not see Janice with him that night.

Mr. Teems stated that on the morning of September 3 between 5:00 and 5:15 a.m., he saw both Danny and Janice at the truck stop. Janice came to his office door and knocked. She asked for money for Danny, and Mr. Teems stated that he was not giving Danny any more money. He stated that Janice had the baby with her and that she replied to him that she would see him tomorrow.

Virginia Brown, a waitress at the Phillips '66, was working third shift on the morning of September 3. She had been working with Danny for about six weeks. At the beginning of her shift at 11 p.m. on September 2, she saw him with Leon Busby and Janice. They came in together and ordered a Coke. During their approximately twenty minutes there, Danny tried to put his arm around both Virginia and the cook on duty. Janice had said to Virginia, "I've been trying to get Danny to bring me up here so I could see what goes on up here." Virginia replied to her, "Well, I don't know what you're talking about; nothing goes on up here."

Virginia stated that she saw Janice later in her shift around 5:15 on the morning of September 3. According to Virginia, Janice came in carrying Alexis and stated that she needed to see the manager to get twenty dollars that he owed Danny. Virginia stated that the manager was upstairs asleep and Janice would have to wake him. She claimed that she gave Alexis some crackers. Janice went up the stairs and came back down stating she couldn't get the manager to wake up. Virginia then had the cook call him on the phone and she gave the phone to Janice. Virginia stated that she talked to the manager on the phone and that he told her to give Janice the money. She gave Janice twenty dollars from the register and she left.

Chambracant Patel, the owner and operator of the Country Boy Inn, testified that Danny and Janice had started out as day to day tenants but evolved into weekly tenants. They were in Room 243 on the back side, closer to Carbondale Road. They had paid their rent on September 1 and this was good until September 8. Demetra Parker resided in Room 253. Mr. Patel had found the key for Room 243 on his desk around 9:30 a.m. on the morning of September 3. That usually indicated to him that a customer had checked out. Demetra, who also paid weekly, was supposed to check out on September 3 and check out time was 11 a.m.

Mr. Patel found the body of Demetra Parker when he went to check on her to see if she was still checking out that morning. When Mr. Patel entered Room 243, he found the room in disarray. No one had bothered the body prior to the arrival of the police. He testified that the Buttrums did not have a car but Demetra did, and that car was missing. He closed the office at 9 p.m. on the evening of September 2, and he did not remember receiving a maintenance call from Miss Henry around 3 a.m. He also did not know how the keys to Room 243 happened to be in his office. On redirect, Mr. Patel stated that Clint McDonald worked for him cleaning rooms but there was no mention of Clint receiving a call during the night.

FBI Special Agent James Sammon from the Pensacola office testified to interviewing Janice after her arrest. He had been with the FBI for twenty-six years and with the Pensacola office for three years. He read Janice her Miranda rights and she signed the form. He interviewed her at 10:57 a.m. and he did not feel that she was under the influence of anything. Janice told him that the tan Buick belonged to Leon Busby. At the time, she denied any involvement in the death of Demetra Parker. Mr. Sammon wrote the statement consulting with Janice sentence by sentence. Janice agreed with the statement and signed it. After Sammon explained that no threats or promises were made to her. The interview lasted approximately two hours and during that time, Mrs. Buttrum never expressed any regret or remorse. Under cross, Agent Sammon said Janice was not cooperative at first, but she was not what he considered hostile or violent.

John Parker, a jailer from the Sheriff's Department, testified to receiving a letter from Janice via the chaplain, Mr. Billy Joe Gibson. He was questioned as to whether or not he had solicited Janice to write this letter. Also, Mr. Parker stated he had spoken to Janice several times a day in his role as a jailer. When Mr. Parker asked Janice about the letter, she said she wanted to make sure it got to the proper authorities.

The letter was then submitted as evidence that Janice had

wanted to take all the blame for the murder of Demetra Parker. This was the letter mentioned earlier, and in it Janice stated that Danny had been coerced into doing what he had done and it was all an act of jealousy. Janice, however, did not take the stand in her own defense. After this witness, the judge sent the jury out for the evening meal. When they returned at 7:30, he decided to postpone closing arguments until the next morning.

The next morning, in his closing argument, DA Williams referred to Danny and Janice as a pair of wolves attacking a sheep in a frenzy. He cited Gregs vs Georgia 428 U.S. 153, "The death penalty is said to serve two principal social purposes: retribution and deterrence of capital crimes by prospective offenders. Mr. Williams referred to Janice as the "Bartow Butcher." He stated that Janice was guilty of the most horrible and heinous crime that one could ever imagine.

Mr. Williams went on to say, "God save us all from the butchering mutilation of human flesh. God save us all from demoralizing indignation of a brutal rape. May Janice Buttrum never again haunt society."

It was interesting to note that both attorneys chose to quote Bible passages in their closing arguments. Mr. Williams chose the passage Romans chapter 13, verse 14 –

> "Let every person be subject to the governing authorities for there is no authority, except from God, and those that exist have been instituted by God. Therefore, he who resists the authorities resists what God has appointed, and those who resist will incur judgment. For rulers are not a terror to good conduct, but to bad. Would you have no fear of him who is in authority? Then do what is good and you will receive his approval.

For he is God's servant for your good, but if you do wrong, be afraid. For he does not bear the sword in vain. He is the servant of God to execute his wrath on the wrongdoer."

Mr. Fain, in his closing argument stated, "But for Danny Buttrum, Demetra Parker would be alive today, but for Danny Buttrum's depraved sexual appetite, we wouldn't be here today."

Mr. Fain went on to describe Janice as a wounded little girl. He chose a scripture from the Old Testament to make his message clear. The verse came from Micah Chapter 6, verse 8, "What doth the Lord require thee, but to justify, and to love mercy. . . to love mercy." He also stated that in Luke Chapter 6, verse 36 it said, "Be merciful, just as your Father is merciful."

Mr. Fain went on to say that God was going to hold Janice Buttrum responsible for what she did. However, these cries for mercy were met with votes of guilty.

Chapter 18

The sentencing phase began immediately after the criminal trial. The state was seeking the death penalty. The prosecuting attorney only called one witness for the state. Mr. Williams would later state that they brought this particular witness in only for Janice's trial and it was his mission to present Janice in the worst possible light.

Mr. Henry Earl Adams was a clinical psychologist. He was employed by the University of Georgia – Athens as a professor, and he also had a part-time private practice. He had published ten books and written over one hundred articles, many of them concerning sexual disorders. His particular interest was sexual deviations, sexual disorders, and criminal behavior.

Mr. Adams reviewed all of the FBI reports concerning Janice: her confessions, reports from Central State Hospital, the autopsy report of Demetra Parker, and the crime scene photos. However, he never talked to Janice personally.

Mr. Adams described Janice as suffering from two distinct psychological conditions. The first, he pointed out, was stimulus hunger. This is defined as an antisocial personality that hungers after stimulation. These individuals are likely to stir up difficulties and get involved in antisocial activities such as drugs and sex in order to excite themselves.

In addition, Mr. Adams stated Janice suffered from polymorphous sexual perversion. This meant that the individual would engage in almost any activity that would turn them on in a sexual nature. This could vary from heterosexual to homosexual in nature. Mr. Adams labeled Janice as having an antisocial personality, as well as being a paraphilia sexual sadist.

Under cross examination, Mr. Greg Brown asked Mr. Adams if he usually performed such explicit and potentially harmful diagnoses or potentially serious diagnoses as he had done on Janice Buttrum on a regular basis, without ever seeing or personally talking to the patient. Mr. Adams answer was that he did and that it was a fairly common practice.

However, in a letter to the DA, Mr. Adams was quoted as saying, "The conclusions that I have reached in this case should be viewed with caution since I have not examined the patient and the evaluation is based largely on her case history that you sent to me."

The first person called by the defense was Harold J. Dale, the mayor of Adairsville from 1976 to 1980. During that time, he presided over traffic court. He had known Danny Buttrum for approximately twenty years. He testified that Danny had a good personality when he was sober, but when he wasn't, he was boisterous, disorderly, and sometimes violent. He had attempted on several occasions to help out Danny.

Ron Jackson was a probation officer for the state of Georgia and was employed in Calhoun, Georgia. He had known Danny for six years. On July 10, 1980, Danny was sentenced to the work camp. Mr. Jackson also noted that on December 16, 1978, Danny was charged with simple battery for beating up Janice. On cross, it was noted that Janice dropped the charges against Danny.

James Edward "Bucky" Crisp had previously spent eight years in law enforcement, but now was a detective in the Gordon County Sheriff's Department. Previously, he had filed charges against Danny for Aggravated Assault. This stemmed from the assault on Devonne Crump with the intent to rape. The charge was reduced to simple battery; however, Mr. Crisp felt the original charge was appropriate.

Jesse Collette was employed with the Department of Offender Rehabilitation Probation at the Rome Diversion Center. In July, 1977, he had a crisis intervention session with Danny Buttrum. Danny came to the Northwest Georgia Regional Hospital in Rome. He felt that Danny needed in-patient services based on statements that Danny had made. He also felt that Danny was becoming schizophrenic and had some paranoid ideations with occasional childish behavior. This was becoming unmanageable at home. His mother, Evelyn, came with him to the hospital. Mr. Collette stated that he considered Danny to be dangerous at that time. On cross, Mr. Williams asked Mr. Collette about Organic Delusional Syndrome. He explained that this can have similar symptoms as schizophrenia and occurs when someone is under the influence of alcohol or drugs. However, Mr. Collette did not feel that Danny was under the influence of alcohol or drugs at that time.

Odell Adcock, a cousin to Mr. Adcock who had raised Janice, testified that he knew both Danny and Janice. He attested to the fact that Danny was violent when he was drunk. Mr. Adcock had issued two different warrants against Danny for beating Janice. He also noted that he believed Janice was in fear of Danny, and he had seen physical marks on her face on one occasion. Danny had also been charged with aggravated battery for beating Gladys Hibbert with an unknown object. There was another peace warrant issued because Gordon Lee Hall was in fear of bodily harm to himself or his family by Danny Buttrum. There was a final peace warrant issued for the same reasons by a man named Tommy Ely.

These peace warrants were the same as what is now known as restraining orders.

Charles B. Jones, the current Justice of the Peace for Adairsville, was called to testify. He stated that he had written two warrants, one in 1977 for Criminal Damage to Property against Danny and one in 1978 for Simply Battery against Janice.

Anthony Atkins, the next door neighbor to Danny and Janice at the Country Boy Inn, took the stand next. He had only talked to the couple on two separate occasions. He saw Danny on the night of September 2 around 8 p.m. and Danny had invited him to the couple's room. Anthony noted that Danny was drinking at the time and he declined the offer. Mr. Atkins was invited to the room a second time around 10 p.m. He again declined the offer by telling Danny that he had to go to work the next day. Danny had a beer in his hand at the time. Anthony was asked by Mr. Fain who the boss was in the relationship and he replied "Danny."

Buford Wayne Phillips stated that he met Danny on the night of September 2, 1980. Buford was in the Mill Creek area at the home of Bob and Vickie Wasserman when Danny came to that residence with Leon Busby. Leon went into the house and tried to get Ann Ray to go with him. Buford stood outside and talked with Danny for about thirty minutes. Buford stated that both Danny and Leon were drinking that night.

Pat Spivey also saw the pair at the Wasserman residence. Ms. Spivey lived in a mobile home next to the Wasserman's. She saw Danny and Janice between 11:00 and 11:30. Pat also stated that Leon was there to see Ann, and she acknowledged that Danny and Leon were drinking.

Pat went on to describe Janice as being very subdued and quiet. Janice had asked Danny's permission before she entered the trailer to get fresh milk for the baby. Pat had worked with Danny for a couple of weeks at the truck stop but she stayed away from him because she thought he was weird. Pat had also served some time in jail with Janice, whom she described as very quiet. She stated that Janice had never shown any homosexual tendencies during that time and that she mentioned several times that she was afraid of Danny. Mr. Fain asked Pat if she thought Janice would commit this crime without severe provocation and she said no.

Mr. Collette was recalled to the stand. This was in regard to Danny's visit in 1977. He stated that Danny came voluntarily and asked for help. He testified that Danny was preoccupied with sex and had hostile feelings towards his mother. He reiterated Mrs. Buttrum's statement about Danny threatening his mother with a butcher knife and scissors. He also stated that Danny appeared to have paranoid feelings and even exhibited hostile feelings toward his mother during the interview. Danny accused his mother of being cruel to his father who died five years ago. (This information was from notes made at Coosa Valley Community Mental Health Center at Northwest Georgia Regional Hospital.)

In an interesting twist, court was held on Sunday afternoon, August 31, 1981. Judge Pannell stated that he did not want to leave the jury with time on their hands, so he asked the jurors if any of them had a problem with continuing court on a Sunday afternoon. None of them objected. He noted that the gallery was full of people from the community who had gone to their respective churches that morning and arrived later in their Sunday best to observe the court proceedings.

Carol Rose was the first witness on that Sunday afternoon. She knew Janice from when she worked at the Bartow County Health Department. Mrs. Rose was employed as a registered nurse and had known Janice since she was five years old. Mrs. Rose knew both Janice's birth mother and the Adcocks. She stated that she had tried to get custody of Janice when Mr. Adcock died, but she was denied because she worked at the Georgia Department of Human Resources. Carol felt that Janice was ill-placed with the Adcocks and that she was very neglected.

Mrs. Tommy West, a librarian at Adairsville Elementary in Bartow County, saw Janice on almost a daily basis and she stated that Janice was usually dirty and smelled bad. She described her hair as being uncombed and that her clothes were too big. Mrs. West had seen her parents pulling clothing out of the trash at the dump. At a hearing on March 17, 1977, she overheard Mrs. Adcock say to Janice that she didn't want to talk to her, she never wanted to see her again and that she didn't want anything to do with her. When asked if Janice had shown signs of any homosexual activity, she replied "No." Mrs. West was also asked if she though Janice was capable of a crime of great violence without outside influence and her reply was again no.

Two former teachers from Adairsville Elementary testified on Janice's behalf. The first was Mary Caruthers. She testified that Janice made good grades, but the other kids wouldn't socialize with her because of her appearance. She described Janice as passive and nonviolent. Mrs. Caruthers claimed to have seen no homosexual activity and did not believe that Janice was capable of a violent crime.

Rose Johnson also described Janice as a quiet child and that she was bullied by other children because of her appearance. She felt that Janice was a follower. She also agreed with Mrs. Caruthers regarding any homosexual activity or propensity to violence.

Marvin Dickerson was a social worker with the Bartow school system. He was a truancy officer and met Janice after she was referred to him because of school attendance issues. He described that when he tried to schedule home visits with the Adcocks that Janice was not present in the home. The trailer was much too small for a family so Janice was living in a van with no wheels in the yard. Every time that he saw Mrs. Adcock she was drunk except for when he took her to court. She noted that Janice was always extremely nice to him and he saw her as a follower. To him, any who treated her with kindness, she reciprocated in kind. On one occasion, Mr. Dickerson overheard Mrs. Adcock tell thirteen-year-old Janice that she hated her and hoped that she never saw her again in her life. He stated that the look on Janice's face was as if someone had thrown a bucket of ice cold water on her. Janice replied to her, "Well, I hate you, too."

Wanda Holstein testified that Janice was part of her case load in April, 1977. She first came to Wanda's attention in October, 1976, when it was alleged that Janice was a deprived child. In October, she was placed in the custody of Bartow County Department of Family and Children Services. They placed her in two foster homes as well as a group home. Although she had no delinquent record, she was then sent to the Macon Youth Developmental Center only because there was nowhere else to put her. When Wanda spoke to Janice, she seemed emotionally immature and had a very low self-image of herself. She did not show any signs of violence. Wanda went on to describe Janice as both a loner and a follower. She thought that Mrs. Adcock tolerated Janice. Mrs. Holstein did not see any homosexual activity nor did she feel that Janice was capable of committing a violent crime.

Glenda Vaughn was a case supervisor with DEFACS. She

also came in contact with Janice in October, 1976. She did a home visit and found filthy conditions. Ms. Vaughn described a home with food that had been sitting around for so long that it had mold on it. Looking for any sign of mother/daughter relationship, Ms. Vaughn noted that she never saw Mrs. Adcock display any physical love towards Janice. She stated that Janice had to be forced to bathe and wash her hair. Ms. Vaughn did not feel that Janice was capable of violence unless she was influenced by others.

Natalin Young was Janice's social worker at Macon YDC. She stated that Janice was there because court services were having a hard time finding a placement. Natalin saw Janice on a daily basis and noted that she did not have many friends. In the beginning, Janice fantasized about her background and often tried to make it sound better than what it actually was. She characterized Janice as quiet and withdrawn.

Mr. Ashley Cox, the Administrator of the Georgia Industrial Home of Macon, Georgia, stated that he met Janice in December, 1977. Under his guardianship for five months, he saw her almost daily. Janice would try to embellish aspects about her life to make it seem better than what it was. Mr. Cox saw Janice as a follower.

Eighteen-year-old Janice took the stand during the sentencing phase. She identified her natural mother as Marie Beavers but she didn't know who her father was. She stated that she was raised by Mr. and Mrs. R.V. Adcock because they had basically paid for her. In describing her home life, Janice said that Mr. Adcock drank on the weekends, but Mrs. Adcock drank on a daily basis. Mrs. Adcock had told Janice that she would be just like her mother. On the weekends, Janice admitted going to the city dump for clothes. Mr. Adcock died on September 10, 1976 and a few weeks later, a new man moved in Mrs. Adcock. Mrs. Adcock often called Janice's mother a tramp and a whore.

Janice met Danny Buttrum on Mother's Day, 1978. A friend of Mrs. Adcock's knew Danny and thought he was running with the wrong crowd. This friend thought Janice might be a good influence on Danny. Only five to six hours after meeting her, Danny decided he wanted to marry Janice. She admitted that she had not had a real boyfriend up to that point. Danny spent the night at the Adcock home and had sex with Janice. They attempted to get married the next day but they were not successful until June 26, 1978. Danny was twenty-six and Janice was only fifteen. This was Danny's second trip to the altar, because he had been previously married and already had two children,

The newlyweds moved around a lot since Danny had trouble holding down a job. Janice stated that when the couple had money that Danny drank. When he was sober, he was quiet. She confessed that he had beaten her at least fifteen times during their short tumultuous marriage. Janice said that Danny would fight with her as if he were fighting with a man. She was pregnant during some of those beatings. Janice had attempted to take out warrants on three separate occasions, but she dropped two and wouldn't testify at the third. She said that he promised that he wouldn't do it anymore, and because she loved him. She had left him on more than one occasion, but he would come to the Adcock home and beg her to take him back. While they were married, he was locked up twice in the Cobb County Work Camp.

On the morning of September 2, 1980, Danny had started drinking between 10:30 and 11:00 a.m. Janice saw Demetra around 11:30 that morning when she went to the store and laundry mat with her. Janice helped Demetra wash and fold clothes. Later in the afternoon, Janice and Danny went over the mountain with Leon Busby to see Ann Ray because he wanted to ask her out. When she asked the purpose of the trip, she was told it was to get Leon a date. The group also went to the Phillip 66 and Amoco truck stops. After they returned to the Country Boy Inn, Danny and Janice borrowed Leon's car and went to Adairsville. They returned to the hotel between 3:00 and 3:30 a.m. on the morning of September 3. She went to Demetra's room to borrow some cigarettes. She returned to Demetra's room because Danny made her.

Janice said that when they returned to Demetra's room that she knocked on the door and Danny stood beside it. When Demetra answered the door, Danny entered the room and Janice stayed outside. After a few minutes, Janice entered the room and since the lights were off, she turned them on. Demetra was on the floor and Danny was removing her panties. Demetra was not struggling, and it appeared to Janice that they were about to have sex. She stood there for what seemed like 2-3 minutes, and then she saw a knife in Danny's hand. Janice took the knife away from him and put it on top of the TV. After she went in the bathroom and came out, she took the knife and attempted to stab Demetra in the heart. Janice claimed that she was hurt and angry.

When Janice was asked if she cut Demetra across the stomach or if she stabbed or hit her anywhere else, she replied no. When asked if she put the toothbrush holder in Demetra's vagina, she said no. She originally had no plans to hurt Demetra until she saw Danny and Demetra together. Janice said that she was sorry for what she had done, and she did feel as if she needed to be punished for what she had done.

After the murder, Janice and Danny took off to Florida

where they were found and arrested. Janice was asked if she recalled telling the FBI agent that she had stabbed Demetra in the vaginal area. She responded that she did tell the agent that but she did not actually commit the act. She also recounted telling authorities that Danny was pleasuring himself while Janice stabbed Demetra. Janice did acknowledge that Danny had sex with Demetra and that he cut her across the stomach. Janice said that the reason she said he didn't was because she wanted to keep him out of jail. She also stated that she did not make Danny do the things he did. As for the letter she had written, Janice testified that she wrote it because she had been pressured by Danny and others to keep Danny out of trouble. She did admit that she was afraid of Danny.

On cross, DA Williams tried to present evidence of the one time that Janice was arrested for striking a police officer, but the judge denied this. Janice also denied helping Danny escape from the work camp. She stated she was picked up after his escape but she did not want to implement the other people involved. Janice denied ever asking Demetra about her sexual preference.

Sheriff Jack Davis was the final witness to testify. He stated that Danny's and Janice's cases were probably the largest ones to have occurred during his administration. He did testify that all mail within the jail was censored. Sheriff Davis did, however, acknowledge that a couple of notes had been sent inside cigarette packs between Danny and Janice, but those had been intercepted. He also stated that when a letter came from the outside, it was checked for anything illegal, passed to the inmate. Once a letter was delivered to an inmate, then the Sheriff would not have the authority to take it back.

Each of the attorneys were allowed to give a closing

argument. DA Williams was first. To quote a passage from the transcript:

> "Consider who was leading who. Who was the worst of the two? Was he coerced into this? Was she really afraid of her husband? She stabbed first. She knocked on the door. She did all the talking and looking for money to get away. She was wearing Demetra's jewelry. Did she ever leave?
>
> How can we feel any sorrow for her, when she cares less about us? Never a word of regret, not the first "I'm sorry." Who will be next? Your wife? Your daughter? Consider who was really leading who? Who did all the action? Consider who was the real worst of the two?
>
> Capital punishment is the ultimate punishment reserved for the ultimate crime. God save us all from Janice Buttrum. May Janice Buttrum never again haunt society.
>
> The defendant has signed her own death warrant. She has brought these proceedings down about her. She has signed her own death warrant. She is responsible for her acts. Now, she is responsible for her death, no one else. I ask you to brand her a butcher."

Mr. Fain argued that Janice should not be convicted of rape. He also stated that Janice did had not have a prior history of criminal activity; this act was committed under the influence of emotional and mental stress. Mr. Fain's pleas of compassion came from his heart. A portion of his closing argument is below.

> "Ladies and Gentleman, in closing, I ask you to care

for Janice Buttrum, care for her as if she were your daughter or your sister who had gotten into the deepest trouble, care for her more than her natural mother did in giving her away, care for her more than her stepmother who rejected her, shunned her, and cursed her, care for her more than Danny Buttrum who beat her and hurt her and led her into this tragedy. I ask you to consider the well-known propositions: Faith, hope, and love. Have faith that all God's creations contains some good. And Janice as God's child, contains that good. Have hope that this goodness which is within Janice will be given the time and the guidance to develop. Have love in your heart for Janice Buttrum who is a human being, who is a little girl - - a little wounded girl who made a foolish, tragic mistake. Ladies and Gentleman, I contend that there is no place in your decision today for vengeance, hatred. Janice Buttrum's life has been filled with hatred, neglect, and vengeance. All but few of society's members have felt like Janice Buttrum belonged and was a part of the trash she - - where she got her clothing. Ladies and Gentleman, I ask you to show Janice that the world is not full of vengeance, but that there is somebody who will take the time to try to understand her, who will care for her, and try to understand her as the little girl that she is. Ladies and Gentleman, I implore you, I plead with you, to have compassion for Janice Buttrum, to give her a chance that she's never had. I ask you to return a sentence, not of death by electrocution, but of life imprisonment. Thank you for your patience and your time. In fact, I know that you will pray deeply from your heart and try to do what is right. Thank you, very much."

It is interesting how living in the Bible belt and quoting scripture played a part in the end results. Ray and Barbara Parker were on hand for the sentencing phase of Janice's trial. Mrs. Parker stated that upon learning about the death of her daughter Demetra, she began to pray for the souls of Danny and Janice Buttrum. She said that she was not bitter about what had happened.

As for Mrs. Parker, an article in the Daily Citizen News, explained what had influenced her to forgive the couple, "When I checked into the room, the Bible was already opened to the 37th chapter of Psalms and was on verses one through nine. I felt that way. I know the sentence won't bring Demetra back either. The scripture said 'the wicked should not be envied their position in life because they will fade away like grass and disappear'. It urges 'trust in the Lord. Be kind and good to others: then you will live safely here in the land and prosper, feeling in safety. He will vindicate you with the blazing light of justice shining down as from the noonday sun."

The jury silently filed out to decide Janice's fate at fifteen minutes before noon. Two hours later, the five women and seven men sentenced Janice to death. Janice sobbed openly as the verdict was read.

Part VI
Life on Death Row and Beyond

Chapter 19

At the time of sentencing, execution was slated for October 19, 1981. The Associated Press stated that Janice Buttrum would become the fourth woman on death row and also the youngest one ever sentenced in the state. Danny had been scheduled to die on August 31, 1981, but it had been delayed since all death penalty cases go through the appeal process sentence. The state Supreme Court was scheduled to hear his case October 10. However, Danny Buttrum had other plans.

In the early morning hours of September 8, Danny Buttrum hanged himself in the Whitfield County Jail. Captain Morris McDonald stated that Danny had fashioned a noose from torn bed sheets. Danny had taken the torn strips and tied one end to the bars above his cell door and the other end became a noose around his neck. He bent his knees and this allowed for enough pressure for asphyxiation.

Danny's lifeless body was found by Deputy Billy Joe Gibson. Deputy Gibson stated that Danny had visited with Janice, their two children and other relatives the previous Sunday afternoon in the chapel. Danny wrote a letter to his wife on Monday and one line of the letter said, "I have little to live for." This meant that Janice was left to await execution alone.

Chapter 20

The Ladies of Death Row

When Janice arrived on death row in Georgia, there were three other women awaiting her arrival and another would soon follow. The inmates were Emma Cunningham, Rebecca Smith Machetti, Shirley Tyler, and Teresa Faye Whittington. Janice mentioned that this group of women was allowed to go out in street clothes and sing at various events. Newspaper articles verified this fact. Janice stated that she sang and played keyboard.

Emma Cunningham, a black woman, was convicted of murder and armed robbery along with her husband James Cunningham. They were indicted for the murder of William Crawford, a white man and a resident of Lincolnton, Georgia. It was January 1, 1979, and Emma and her husband had been washing clothes in the local African American laundry mat called the Washhouse. After the clothes were washed, the couple walked to Emma's father's house, which was near Mr. Crawford's home, where they asked Emma's father to drive them home. According to Emma, after she and James arrived home, James left and returned around 1 a.m. shaking Emma awake and telling her they had to leave. The couple escaped to Augusta and when they returned to their home, James was arrested. He quickly included his wife in his confession, although it was never proven that Emma was a participant in the crime. Emma was given a new trial in 1982 and at her new trial she was given a life sentence. Just prior to her release, she began a career as a gospel singer. Within a year of her release in 1990, she was diagnosed with lupus and suffered heart problems.

Rebecca Smith Machetti was sentenced to execution in 1974 for the murder of her ex-husband and his new wife. The murders occurred so that family members could collect insurance benefits. She was granted a new trial, and her sentence was changed to two life terms in 1983. Eventually she was paroled in 2009 at the age of 71.

The third occupant of death row, Teresa Faye Whittington, was convicted of the 1982 murder of Cheryl Marie Soto. Teresa became acquainted with Rick Soto through her job at a local Starvin' Marvin convenience store in October, 1981. The pair began dating and Rick convinced Teresa to help him kill his wife. Rick and Teresa shot Cheryl twice while she was bathing in the couple's home. A plugged-in radio was then thrown into the bathtub. Mrs. Soto was three months pregnant at her death. Teresa was sent to death row in 1982 but was granted a new trial. She too left the confines of death row.

Shirley Tyler was the fourth women on death row. She was sentenced to death for the 1979 poisoning death of her husband. She poisoned his chili with a powder used to kill roaches supposedly because she was afraid he would do physical harm to her son. Mr. Tyler had a history of abuse in the past. Both Mr. and Mrs. Tyler were black and the black community was outraged over the incident so no one wanted to testify on Mrs. Tyler's behalf. Mrs. Tyler won an appeal and was granted a new trial. One basis for this was that her attorney had just pass the bar and had no legal experience when he was assigned Mrs. Tyler's case.

Janice soon found herself alone. When asked what it was

like when the final person left, Janice said it was like losing her family. These women had spent twenty-four hours a day, seven days a week together, so in a sense, they were family.

Chapter 21

Appeal Process – Buttrum v. The State

Every person who is sentenced for a crime has the right to appeal his or her verdict. Janice's first appeal occurred in April, 1982, when her case was heard by the State Supreme Court. The defendant has the opportunity to submit errors that he/she feels occurred during his/her trial as a means of the higher court considering the possibility for a change in the lower court's ruling.

In Janice's case, the court first dealt with was errors 3 and 4. These were errors that her attorney felt had occurred during the trial process. Errors three and four were that the trial court erred in Janice's motion for a change of venue and also failed to disqualify two jurors who had already formed an opinion of guilt. Janice felt that, because of all the pretrial publicity, a fair trial was impossible. The court found no merit to these errors.

Error 5 stated that the court erred in allowing evidence from Janice's hotel room, statements from arresting officers, and evidence from Demetra's car. Janice stated that the rent on the room at the Country Boy Inn had been paid up through September 8. Therefore, when officers entered the room on September 3, Danny and Janice were still in possession of the room. However, the owner of the hotel found the room key on the desk in his office, and he concluded that the couple had abandoned the room.

Errors 6 and 7 stated that the court erred when it stated

that Janice should have the burden of proof as to her plea of mental incompetence. The document also stated that the court should have used the word competency instead of sanity when he charged the jury.

Error 8 probably had the biggest impact. With this error, Janice stated that the court erred when they denied funds to the defendant's attorneys to employ a psychiatrist, field investigator, and forensic criminologist. In Sabel v. State , 248 Ga. 10 (6) (282 SE2d 61) (1981), it states "A criminal defendant on trial for his liberty is entitled on motion timely made to have an expert of his choosing, bound by appropriate safeguards imposed by the court, examine critical evidence whose nature is subject to varying expert opinion."

In error 9, Janice stated that the letter she wrote while incarceration to the jailer at Whitfield County Jail claiming that Danny was not responsible for the crime should not have been allowed in her trial.

The number one error of the filing contended that the court erred when they allowed the testimony of Dr. Henry Adams. An expert witness may only give his opinion based on facts. Dr. Adams had never personally spoken to Janice so his opinion would only be based on partial facts.

After sentence review, the court stated that the crimes of Janice Buttrum could only be described as butchery and barbarism. They determined that the death sentence was neither excessive nor disproportionate. They confirmed the prior judgment.

Chapter 22

Buttrum vs Black

Janice soon found her case going up the ladder of justice. In September, 1989, the case of Janice Buttrum vs Gary Black came before the United States District Court in Rome. Gary Black was the warden of the Middle Georgia Correctional Institute. Janice filed a petition for habeas corpus relief. She was asking for her murder conviction to be lifted and for relief from her death sentence.

The first section of the petition dealt with procedural and factual history. It basically summarized what had happened in regard to Janice's initial conviction as well as the facts of the murder of Demetra Parker. This section also addressed the personal life history of Janice.

Section Two addressed Constitutional Challenges in the Guilt/Innocence Phase of the trial. This section again addressed widespread pretrial publicity that had occurred. Some things that were addressed were death threats and preconceived ideas of guilt in the community. Janice's attorneys provided pages of examples from the local media that depicted the couple in a negative light. These remarks were made before, during, and after the various trials.

The Sentencing Phase was under scrutiny in section three. This probably dealt with the biggest issue of the constitutionality of executing someone who was seventeen at the time of the crime. Evidence submitted suggested an emotional maturity of someone twelve to thirteen years old. Up to this point the United States had executed only nine females who had committed crimes before their 18th birthday. The last such execution occurred in 1912. It was also stated that over 2,000 females were presently on death row and only two were minors at the time of their crime.

Section Three also addressed again the testimony of Dr. Henry Adams. He was the psychologist brought in by the prosecution during the sentencing phase to give his opinions regarding Janice. Dr. Adams would testify to the fact he had never spoken to Janice and based his opinion solely on case files. Janice introduced affidavits from three different psychiatrists who had evaluated her. All three of them felt that Janice was wrongly labeled as a sexual sadist. Janice did not have a history of sexual crimes; however, Danny's history revealed an urge to rape women and homicidal urges. The attorneys also addressed the fact that Janice's legal team had not been given funds to acquire their own experts. Their request for funds had been denied.

The court's ruling was as follows: "According, Petitioner Buttrum's petition for Writ of Habeas Corpus is granted in part and denied in part. The writ of Habeas Corpus is denied as to her conviction of murder and it is granted as to the sentence of death. Respondent Black is ordered to grant the petitioner a new sentencing hearing to commence within six months from the date of this order, or if an appeal is taken from this order, within six months of the date this order becomes final. The order was dated the 20th day of September, 1989."

Basically this meant, Janice would no longer find herself on death row. There was a small speck of light at the end of a very long tunnel.

Chapter 23

Partain Agreement – 1991

Through the various appeals processes, Janice had been represented by George Kendall, an attorney for the NAACP Legal Defense Fund. Any person who is sentenced to execution has the right to legal representation from someone in this group. Beginning in April, 1980, Mr. Kendall sent several letters to Jack Partain, District Attorney for Whitfield County, and Kermit McManus, Assistant District Attorney.

Jack Partain had served as Assistant District Attorney under Steve Williams, who was responsible for prosecuting Danny and Janice Buttrum. Jack began working for the DA's office in July, 1980, just three months prior to the murder at the Country Boy Inn. He had served as an attorney in the Atlanta area and had defended several death penalty cases.

The initial letter was a follow-up to a discussion between the parties regarding the possibility of avoiding a second trial for Janice. Mr. Kendall stressed that under Georgia law, he could guarantee Janice would serve at least twenty years. He referenced O.C.G.A. §42-9-39 (c) which stated,

> "*When a person receives consecutive life sentences as the result of offenses occurring in the same series of acts and any one of the life sentences is imposed for the crime of murder, such person shall serve consecutive ten year periods for each such sentence, up to a maximum of 30 years,* before being eligible for

parole consideration."

Mr. Kendall went on to say that consecutive life sentences were a harsh punishment. He compared Janice's case with a more notorious Georgia case. "Two of three Alday killers – each of whom was convicted of six murders – received consecutive life sentences. Only Carl Issacs was resentenced to death. McClendon and Westbrook who killed four and two persons respectively each received consecutive life sentences. While you and I agree that Ms. Buttrum's crime was horrendous, it was no more aggravated than these other cases and involved fewer victims."

Finally, Mr. Kendall stressed that the state of Georgia had never executed a juvenile female, regardless of her crime. He stated, "I suspect that Whitfield County would prefer to catapult itself before the nation and world in ways other than to become known as the jurisdiction in the United States that broke the near century-long moratorium on executing juvenile female offenders."

In the second letter, Mr. Kendall stressed that he hoped the trio could agree to a settlement that would assure a long period of incarceration in place of there being a trial. He did not deny the seriousness of the crime committed but felt that the death penalty should be reserved for hardened psychopaths such as Ted Bundy or Carl Issacs. He also stated that Janice would waive her rights if an agreement to consecutive life sentences could be reached.

Mr. Kendall and Mr. Partain had been looking at their options in regards to Janice's case. In the final letter, Mr. Kendall stated that he strongly felt that the death penalty should be removed from the equation and instead consecutive life sentences be considered. He asked that Mr. Partain and Mr. McManus give considerable weight to Janice's age at the time of the crime. Mr. Kendall stated, “Society requires that those of us in the criminal justice system treat adolescents differently than adults.”

Mr. Kendall stressed the fact that the state of Georgia recognized the age of maturity as eighteen. This meant that a person younger than that would be considered ill prepared to handle the full responsibility of adulthood. He also stressed to Mr. Partain and Mr. McManus the things a person was prohibited to do who was under the age of eighteen. A minor is unable to vote, serve on a jury, obtain a driver’s license without parental consent, and obtain a carry permit for a weapon. In addition to that, they are unable to purchase alcohol, donate an organ, or hold many types of public office.

It was expressed that various judicial organizations opposed capital punishment for minors. These groups felt that eighteen should be the minimal age. Mr. Kendall even went as far as to say if Janice had committed her crime in the Soviet Union, China, South Africa, or Iraq, she would not be facing the death penalty.

The final decision was left to Mr. Partain to make. It must have felt as if the weight of the world was resting on his shoulders. He had to determine what was in the best interest of all the parties involved. He had to make sure Janice paid the price for her crime and the Parkers received justice for Demetra.

A decision was finally reached in June, 1991. A two-page press release summed up the decisions that had been made. The press release is featured below:

Press Release

Buttrum Pleads Guilty to Charges, Life Imprisonment without Parole

Dalton, GA – Janice Marie Buttrum pleaded guilty today to charges of armed robbery and rape in the 1980 torture slaying of a Tennessee teenager, and was sentenced to three consecutive life terms in prison without parole.

Buttrum was found guilty by a jury of murder and theft in her trial in 1981, and was sentenced to death in the electric chair. The original sentence was overturned by the Federal District Court, and a new sentencing trial was scheduled to take place in August.

"Make no mistake; we believe that the correct punishment for Mrs. Buttrum is execution by electrocution, and we deeply regret that her original sentence was reversed by the Federal Courts," said District Attorney Jack Partain. "We believe that this negotiated sentence, in which Mrs. Buttrum pleads guilty to two additional charges and agrees that she will spend the rest of her natural life in prison, with no chance of parole best serves the purpose of the family of her victim, and the citizens of the State of Georgia.

He said that the fact that Mrs. Buttrum was a teenager at the time the crimes were committed, and that she is female, would make it highly unlikely that she would ever be executed. This feeling is shared by the family of the victim, and they are supportive of this disposition of the case, Partain said. "This disposition spares the family of the agony of another trial."

He added that if the resentencing phase of the trial resulted in a verdict of life imprisonment that Mrs. Buttrum would be immediately eligible for parole because of the time she has served in prison already, a fact that could not be shared with a jury.

"The terms of the contract Mrs. Buttrum has entered into with the State are very specific," Partain said. "She agrees to plead guilty to two additional charges; she agrees to a sentence of three consecutive life terms in prison, and she agrees to waive forever any right she might hold to parole from the state of Georgia.

"Our interest is in ensuring that for as long as she lives, Janice Buttrum never again poses a threat to our society, and this agreement does just that."

Chapter 24

Life in Prison

After Janice was given the chance at a new trial, she was allowed to leave death row at Hardwick. Through the years, she has been incarcerated at various prisons throughout Georgia. People are left to wonder if life in prison really changed Janice.

Janice has stated that she was in her early 20's before she realized that Danny Buttrum never really loved her. By then, she had lost both her children to the Buttrum family and was sitting alone on death row. She lives with many regrets. One of those is having taken a human life. Many times she has said she would gladly give her own life if it would bring Demetra Parker back.

Janice has tried to make the most of her time behind bars. She has pursued a college education and works a full-time job. She has sought out support groups to try to pick up the pieces of her broken life. Not long after her incarceration and while still housed in Whitfield County, she was visited by Demetra Parker's mother. Mrs. Parker stated that she forgave Janice for what had happened. Shortly before her death, Elizabeth Adcock also visited Janice in prison and the pair was able to make amends.

Thirty-six years have passed since Janice was first incarcerated. So many things have changed in the modern world since then. She admitted she had never been in a Walmart store. There were no such things as cell phones, the internet or even 911. If a person needed to find out what something was, one trusted the World Book Encyclopedia would have the answers.

Janice has suffered personal loss herself. It has been over ten years since she has seen her two daughters. She also has five grandchildren she has never seen. Janice lives with what she calls the "woulda, coulda, shoulda" moments. So many things would be different. The prison system offers classes for "lifers" in order to teach them what to expect if they ever have the chance to enter back into civilization. Janice completed that class in 2016 and each participant is required to speak about his/her experience. Here is what she had to say about her experience:

"My name is Janice Buttrum and my talk is about 'Stepping out of my Comfort Zone.'

Everything bad in my life happened in September. My father died in 1976, my crime occurred, and my husband and codefendant committed suicide.

Every year I'd distance myself from everyone for the entire month of September because I couldn't bear to lose anyone else in that awful month.

In 2009, a very close lifer friend pulled me out of that cycle. She told me that GOD had given me 12 months to be joyful and not 11 months.

So I started playing Scrabble and going outside with people.

Now I remember all the good things that happened in September. My death sentence got overturned, the birth of my beautiful granddaughter and now Graduation from this wonderful group.

This group has taught me how to be myself and never feel

like I don't matter. Our wonderful leader Mrs. Jackson, who has shown us she truly cares about us and my new sisters who always have my back.

I now have the courage to be myself and not what others would like me to be.

In conclusion, GOD has taken a "Bad Month" and turned it into a month of JOY for me.

I am now free and out of my comfort zone!

Psalms chapter 30, verse 5, section b – weeping may stay for the night, but rejoicing comes in the morning."

Chapter 25

The Light at the End of the Tunnel

In 2012, the United States Supreme Court ruled on the case of Miller vs. Alabama. The ruling stated that state and the federal government are required to consider the unique circumstances of each juvenile defendant when determining each individual's sentence.

This case involved a young man named Evan Miller. In July, 2003, Evan, along with Colby Smith, killed a young man named Cole Cannon by beating him with a bat and then setting his mobile home on fire. Miller was 14-years-old at the time of the crime. At his trial, he was sentenced to life in prison without the possibility of parole. Miller petitioned for a new trial on the basis that his sentence constituted cruel and unusual punishment.

In a 5-4 ruling by the Supreme Court, the Court ruled that the 8th Amendment to the Constitution prohibits cruel and unusual punishment and that a mandatory sentence of life in prison without the possibility of parole for juvenile homicide offenders is forbidden. Basically, they determined that children are different from adults when it comes to sentencing. The 8th Amendment is not violated when it comes to adults but would be unconstitutional when applied to juveniles.

In 2016, the Supreme Court case of Montgomery vs. Louisiana brought further clarification to the previous ruling made in 2012. The case involved Henry Montgomery. He was convicted of murder and received the death penalty for a murder that occurred in 1963. At the time of the murder, Henry had just turned 17 years old. Henry appealed his conviction to the Louisiana Supreme court and his conviction was overturned. At a new trial, he was again convicted, but this time he was sentenced to life without parole.

Due to the Supreme Court ruling in the 2012 case of Miller vs. Alabama, it was decided that juveniles could not be sentenced to life without parole because this violated the 8th Amendment. Because of this decision, Henry filed a motion arguing that he had received an illegal sentence. The Supreme Court ruled 6-3 that when a Court establishes a constitutional rule, that this rule must apply retroactively.

One must wonder, how this case affects Janice Buttrum. As of this writing, that decision remains in the balance. Discussions are being considered which would allow Janice's sentence of life without the possibility of parole to be changed to a life sentence with the possibility of parole. This would fall under the Montgomery ruling and allow Janice the chance at a parole hearing. Does this mean Janice will walk out a free woman? That is something only time will tell.

Index

CPSIA information can be obtained
at www.ICGtesting.com
Printed in the USA
LVOW12s1531070917
547903LV00003B/597/P

9 781478 790495